Air Fryer Accessories Recipe Cookbook

# Legal

**DISCLAIMER:** This book is independently published by, and is **not** affiliated with, sponsored by, or endorsed by any of the products mentioned in this book. All other company and product names are the trademarks of their respective owners.

This information contained in this book is for entertainment purposes only. The content represents the opinion of the author and is based on the author's personal experience and observations. The author does not assume any liability whatsoever for the use of or inability to use any or all information contained in this book, and accepts no responsibility for any loss or damages of any kind that may be incurred by the reader as a result of actions arising from the use of the information in this book. Use this information at your own risk. No part of this book may be reproduced or transmitted in any form or by any means, electronic or mechanical, including photocopying, recording, or by any information storage or retrieval system, without express written permission from the author, except in the case of brief quotations embodied in critical articles and reviews – or except by a reviewer who may quote brief passages in a review.

Respective authors hold all copyrights not held by the publisher

---

**NOTE:** Some of the recipes in this book include raw eggs. Raw eggs may contain bacteria. It is recommended that you purchase certified salmonella-free eggs from a reliable source and store them in the refrigerator. You should not feed raw eggs to babies or small kids. Likewise, pregnant women, elderly persons, or those with a compromised immune system should not eat raw eggs. Neither the author nor the publisher claims responsibility for adverse effects resulting from the use of the recipes and/or information found within this book.

---

The author reserves the right to make any changes he or she deems necessary to future versions of the publication to ensure its accuracy.

COPYRIGHT © 2018, All Rights Reserved.

Published in The United States of America

By Alicia Patterson

# Introduction

Step up your game and get frying with these air fryer recipes that are **made with the air fryer accessories. A must-have asset** to have as a part of your recipe playbook in preparing food in your kitchen. We've made it easy to follow and great to eat! We understand that everyone has lives and such a busy schedule that lots of families don't even have time to cook anymore. That's why this book is a must have for your kitchen.

Let's admit one thing here...**Air Fryer Accessories just make cooking better.** That's just what they do! And we've added these hand selected menu items for your devouring needs. Just imagine, coming home from work and not having time to cook being a "thing-of-the-past!" Just putting in the food and turning on the machine.

We've found that there are specific settings within the air fryer controls that make this device easy for anyone to cook up something delicious. Most of these recipes inside of this book are very healthy indeed! We always want to keep in account that there are a lot of families that want to eat as clean as they can and healthy.

*BONUS: we've also included some cool cooking charts and "mouth-watering" marinades that will make the juices of the meat and veggies you are preparing, melt in your mouth.*

Your kids will have so much fun helping you cook in the kitchen. So put those kiddos to work and get them helping out in the kitchen with you!

Air Fryer Accessories Recipe Cookbook

# Table of Contents

| | |
|---|---|
| LEGAL | 2 |
| INTRODUCTION | 3 |
| TABLE OF CONTENTS | 4 |
| MEET THE AIR FRYER ACCESSORIES | 6 |
| Enhancing The Food Making Experience | 6 |
| VARIOUS PARTS OF MOST AIR FRYERS | 8 |
| All the Features You Need | 8 |
| USING YOUR AIR FRYER | 9 |
| The 11 Simple Steps of Most General Air Fryers | 9 |
| CLEANING IS EASY AS 1-2-3 | 10 |
| Keeping Your Air Fryer & Accessories Clean | 10 |
| AIR FRYER 101 | 11 |
| Optimize the Use of Your Air Fryer | 11 |
| GET READY TO START AIR FRYING! | 12 |
| BEEF | 13 |
| Beef Stir Fry | 14 |
| Beef Taco Eggrolls | 15 |
| Mongolian Beef with Green Beans | 16 |
| Beef Fried Rice | 17 |
| Beef Meatballs | 18 |
| Carne Asada Tacos | 19 |
| Chicken Fried Steak | 20 |
| Beef Stuffed Roasted Bell Peppers | 21 |
| Mini Meatloaf | 22 |
| BBQ Bourbon Bacon Burger | 23 |
| CHICKEN | 24 |
| Chicken Parm | 25 |
| Honey Sriracha Hot Wings | 26 |
| Tandoori Chicken | 27 |
| Parmesan Garlic Chicken Wings | 28 |
| Parmesan Garlic Chicken Tenders | 29 |
| Pizza Stuffed Chicken Thighs | 30 |
| Thai Chicken Eggrolls | 31 |
| Chicken Nuggets | 32 |
| Roast Chicken | 33 |
| Classic Fried Chicken Thighs | 34 |
| Nashville Hot Fried Chicken | 35 |
| Honey Garlic Chicken Wings | 36 |
| Crispy Restaurant Style Chicken Sandwiches | 37 |
| BBQ Chicken | 38 |
| Spicy BBQ Chicken | 39 |

| | |
|---|---|
| Crispy Chicken Breast | 40 |
| Crispy Spicy Chicken Breast | 41 |
| Jerk Chicken Wings | 42 |
| Bloody Mary Wings | 43 |
| Buffalo Wings | 44 |
| Delicious Honey Dijon Wings | 45 |
| Spicy Peach Chicken Wings | 46 |
| Cilantro Lime Chicken Wings | 47 |
| Mongolian Chicken Wings | 48 |
| Root Beer BBQ Wings | 49 |
| Balsamic Glazed Wings | 50 |
| Korean BBQ Wings | 51 |
| Jack Daniels BBQ Wings | 52 |
| PORK | 53 |
| Breaded Pork Chops | 54 |
| Parmesan Crusted Pork Chops | 55 |
| Garlic Butter Pork Chops | 56 |
| Bacon Wrapped Pork Tenderloin with Apples and Gravy | 57 |
| Easy Pork Taquitos | 58 |
| Bacon Wrapped Cajun Jalapeños | 59 |
| Bacon Wrapped Shrimp Jalapeños | 60 |
| SEAFOOD | 61 |
| Spicy Crunchy Shrimp | 62 |
| Cajun Shrimp | 63 |
| Crispy Coconut Shrimp with Spicy Citrus Sauce | 64 |
| Sweet Citrus Salmon | 65 |
| Soy Lemon Sugar Salmon | 66 |
| Crab Cake Sliders | 67 |
| Crab Fried Rice | 68 |
| Lobster Tails with Lemon Garlic Butter | 69 |
| Keto Friendly Shrimp Scampi | 70 |
| Bacon Wrapped Scallops | 71 |
| BEFORE YOU GO FURTHER! | 72 |
| We Need Your Help... ☺ | 72 |
| SIDES | 73 |
| Asparagus with Basil & Olive Oil | 74 |
| Asparagus with Lemon Pepper | 75 |
| Asparagus with Carrots | 76 |
| Honey Carrots | 77 |
| Asian Cauliflower Carrots | 78 |
| Fried Pickles | 79 |
| Garlic Fried Pickles | 80 |
| Spicy Fried Pickles | 81 |
| Golden Crisp French Fries | 82 |
| Golden Scallion Garlic Fries | 83 |

By Alicia Patterson

| | |
|---|---|
| Parmesan Fries | 84 |
| Garlic Parmesan Fries | 85 |
| Garlic Parmesan Jalapeño Fries | 86 |
| Sweet Potato Fries | 87 |
| Spicy Sweet Potato Fries | 88 |
| Truffle Parmesan Fries | 89 |
| Garlic Parmesan Roasted Potatoes | 90 |
| Turmeric Tofu and Cauliflower Rice | 91 |
| Fried Ravioli with Marinara Sauce | 92 |
| Avocado Fries with Lime Dip | 93 |
| Stuffed Mushrooms | 94 |
| Honey Glazed Button Mushrooms | 95 |
| Zucchini Fries | 96 |
| Shishito Peppers with Asiago Cheese | 97 |
| Salt & Vinegar Chips | 98 |
| Beet Chips | 99 |
| Potato Chips | 100 |
| Parmesan Potato Chips | 101 |
| Garlic Parmesan Potato Chips | 102 |
| Fried Green Tomatoes with Sriracha Mayonnaise | |
| Dipping Sauce | 103 |
| Roasted Chickpeas | 104 |
| Plantain Chips | 105 |
| Buffalo Cauliflower | 106 |
| Popcorn tofu with Sriracha Mayo | 107 |
| Taco Matzo Chips | 108 |
| Apple Chips | 109 |
| Patatas Bravas | 110 |
| Fried Guacamole Balls | 111 |
| Onion Roasted Potatoes | 112 |
| Corn Tortilla Chips | 113 |
| Parmesan Zucchini Chips | 114 |
| Broccoli with Cheese Sauce | 115 |

## EGGS 116

| | |
|---|---|
| Hard Boiled Eggs | 117 |
| Two Egg Omelet | 118 |
| Fried Eggs | 119 |
| Shirred Eggs | 120 |
| Soft Boiled Eggs | 121 |
| Baked Eggs | 122 |
| Eggs In A Mini Bread Bowl | 123 |
| Scrambled Eggs | 124 |
| Breakfast Soufflé | 125 |
| Scotch Eggs | 126 |
| Ham and Eggs Toast Cups | 127 |
| Chorizo and Potato Frittata | 128 |
| Spinach and Sausage Egg Cups | 129 |
| Avocado Egg Cups | 130 |
| Portobello and Parmesan Egg Cups | 131 |

## BREAKFAST 132

| | |
|---|---|
| Pancakes | 133 |
| German Pancakes | 134 |
| French Toast Sticks | 135 |
| Lemon Blueberry Muffins | 136 |
| Cinnamon Crumb Coffee Cake Muffins | 137 |
| Potato and Tofu Scramble | 138 |
| French Toast | 139 |
| Paleo Pumpkin Muffins | 140 |
| Easy Donuts | 141 |
| Baked Oatmeal | 142 |

## DESSERT 143

| | |
|---|---|
| Apple Fries with Whip Cream Caramel Sauce | 144 |
| Peanut Butter and Banana Bites | 145 |
| Nutella and Banana Sandwiches | 146 |
| Double Chocolate Brownies | 147 |
| Caramel Popcorn | 148 |
| Banana Churro | 149 |
| Popcorn | 150 |
| Caramel Popcorn | 151 |
| Apple Dumplings | 152 |
| Fruit Crumble Mug Cake | 153 |
| Chocolate Cake | 154 |
| Baked Apple | 155 |
| Shortbread Cookies | 156 |
| Fried Banana S'more | 157 |
| Mini Apple Pies | 158 |
| Chocolate M&M Cookies | 159 |

## PIZZA 160

| | |
|---|---|
| Pita Bread Cheese Pizza | 161 |
| Caprese Pizza | 162 |
| Indian Spiced Turkey & Broccoli Pizza | 163 |
| The Mafia Mangler Pizza | 164 |
| The "Big Tony" Pizza | 165 |
| The "Hot Meathead" Pizza | 166 |

## WHAT'S NEXT ON THE LIST! 167

| | |
|---|---|
| Review Time... ☺ | 167 |

## YOURS FOR LOOKING 168

| | |
|---|---|
| "BONUS" Get Your Air Fryer Marinades for Meats & Veggies Now! | 168 |
| Metric Volume Conversions Chart | 169 |
| Metric Weight Conversion Chart | 170 |
| Temperature Conversion Chart | 170 |
| Food Temperatures for Safe Heating, Danger Chilling & Freezing Zones! | 171 |
| Air Fryer Creation Recipes & Notes: | 172 |

## ABOUT THE AUTHOR 173

Air Fryer Accessories Recipe Cookbook

# Meet The Air Fryer Accessories

## Enhancing The Food Making Experience

There are many air fryer accessories on the market today. The ones that we are using here in this book are completely compatible with a lot of air fryers. These air fryer accessories are completely universal, fitting any 3.7quart air fryer. They work very well with any Phillips, Gowise, Cozyna, and Power air fryer.

**This air fryer accessory kit we used in this book features six pieces:** The kit is comprised of one metal holder, one pizza pan, one fewer rack, one metal holder, One silicon mat, and one mini cakes silicone pan.

**Cook more things with this air fryer accessory:** The kit allows you to expand the capabilities of your air fryer. Make delicious cakes with the cake barrel, bake mouthwatering pizza with the pizza pan, prepare more food with the metal holder, and cook delicious kebabs and skewers with the skewer rack.

**Easy clean up:** All of the air fryer accessories can be placed in your dishwasher to make cleaning a breeze.

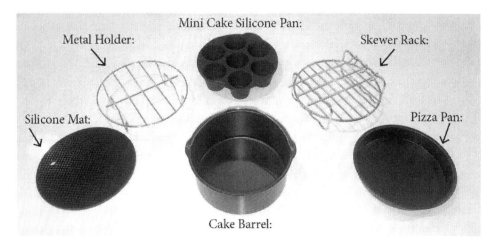

By Alicia Patterson

**Pizza Pan:** The pizza pan is obviously the perfect way to bake delicious pizza but it's great for other foods too. Make scrumptious cookies, potatoes, egg dishes, and even pancakes with it.

**Metal Holder:** The metal holder allows you to cook more in your air fryer. It gives you a second layer to place food on so you can maximize space.

**Skewer Rack:** The skewer rack is a dual threat in your air fryer. You can use it to cook three skewers and you can use the wire rack below to cook your favorite side at the same time.

**Cake Barrel:** The cake barrel gives you the freedom to bake your favorite cakes and breads in your air fryer. The barrel transfers heat evenly so your baked goods turn out perfect every time.

**Silicone Mat:** The silicone mat protects the surfaces in your kitchen. The mat is heat resistant and is the perfect place to put your hot accessories when you take them out of your air fryer.

**Mini Cake Silicone Pan:** Some accessories depending on which you buy will even come with a mini cake silicone pan is the perfect way to bake muffins and cupcakes. Pour the batter directly into the molds and watch as the air fryer bakes them to perfection.

Air Fryer Accessories Recipe Cookbook

# Various Parts of Most Air Fryers

## All the Features You Need

We've found that most air fryers are built with multiple features to make cooking not only convenient, but a breeze.

**Control Panel:** Most air fryers have a control panel has presets that cook foods like chicken, shrimp, and beef at specific temperatures for the predetermined time to give you perfect results. You can also set the timer temperature manually with plus or mind buttons next to clearly marked time and temperature icons.

**Fryer Basket:** Most all air fryers will come with a detachable fryer basket, so that you can easily pour out your food without excess oil dripping on it. Some of them come equipped with a release button to keep the oil from spilling out of the pan.

**Pan:** A lot of air fryers have the nonstick pan that can be detached from the fryer basket, and catches all the oil that drips through the holes in the basket

**Presets:** Some air fryers may come equipped with various presets to make cooking easy. You have presets for fries, chicken, steak, shrimp, pork, cake, fish, and warm. The warm preset warms food for a few minutes making it great for reheating things.

**LCD:** A lot of air fryers come equipped with some kind of LCD screen which lets you know what presets you're using if you decide to go that route. It also tells you the temperature and cooking time.

By Alicia Patterson

# Using Your Air Fryer

## The 11 Simple Steps of Most General Air Fryers

1. Always have your air fryer on an even and flat surface when using it. The fryer needs to be on a heat resistant surface, (such as the silicone mat) because it gets hot and can melt things.

2. Attach the basket to the pan. (if basket doesn't attach...next step)

3. Put whatever ingredients you're using into the basket and then place the attached basket and pan in the air fryer... push the start button.

4. Choose either one of the presets or set the temperature and cooking time manually using the plus and minus buttons or with a knob control.

5. When everything is set, push start again, to start the cooking process.

6. On a lot of air fryers, when the cooking process starts you'll see an indicator light blink. This means the temperature is rising and hot air is moving around and circulating.

7. Some recipes ask you to flip the food or shake the basket during the cooking process. You need to pull out the pan using the handle and gently shake it. Make sure you don't press the basket release button while shaking the basket and pan.

8. When some air fryer machines are done cooking your food it will make beep or let you know in some sort of way. On some air fryers the fan icon will also turn off when done. (check to see if this is the case on your air fryer.)

9. Gently remove the pan with basket attached and put the pan down on a pot holder.

10. On some air fryers models, you will have the hold the release button down on the fryer basket and pull the handle to remove the basket.

11. Place the cooked food on a plate or in a bowl to serve.

Air Fryer Accessories Recipe Cookbook

# Cleaning is Easy As 1-2-3

## Keeping Your Air Fryer & Accessories Clean

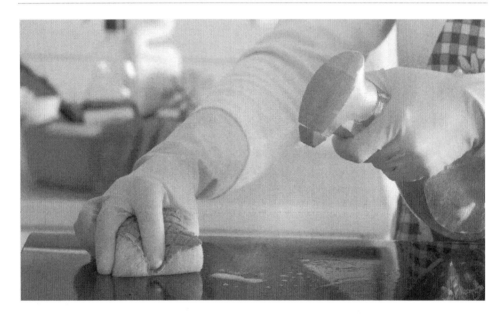

We've found that cleaning your Air Fryer and all Air Fryer Accessories is not only incredibly simple, but easier than we expected. Make sure you wait until your air fryer has cooled off before cleaning it. Do the same for the accessories. Use a moist towel to clean off the outside parts(s) of the fryer and accessories. Use either a slightly wet non-abrasive cloth or sponge to clean the inside of the accessories and fryer.

If you want to clean the heating coil of your air fryer, use a cleaning brush to gently get rid of any debris. Use hot water, a non-abrasive sponge, and some soap to get the basket and pan clean. If you have food debris stuck on either use a little degreasing dish soap. If there's anything that is really stuck on particles in the pan, soak it in hot water for a while. You can place the basket in your dishwasher, but you must remove the handle using a wrench to get the bolts loose so you can remove the screws. **These air fryer handles usually aren't dishwasher safe.**

By Alicia Patterson

# Air Fryer 101

## Optimize the Use of Your Air Fryer

- If you like your food really crispy...Get a kitchen spray bottle. It's easier to spray your food with oil than coating it with any other method. Spray bottles disperse oil better so you don't need to use as much to coat your food.
- Put a little oil in the pan when you cook foods with high fat. This is something you should use for food like sausage and bacon because it helps to stop the grease that drips down from smoking.

- Ideally let food come up to room temperature before placing it in your air fryer. Room temperature food cooks faster and ends up crispier than foods that are colder.

- Use parchment paper or aluminum for oil for easier basket cleanup your parchment paper or aluminum foil for easier basket cleanup. Make sure that the aluminum foil or parchment paper doesn't cover the entire bottom of the basket because this will restrict airflow and stop your food cooking properly.

- Shake the basket. Shaking your basket during the cooking process allows the food to cook more evenly.

- Don't overfill your basket. Overfilling your basket won't get enough heat flowing to the food to cook evenly. Food will take longer to cook, and won't end up as crispy.

- Try using the settings that are pre-set for different foods such as: fries, chicken, steak, shrimp, fish, pork, cake, pork and cake. There is even a warm setting to keep your food warm.

Air Fryer Accessories Recipe Cookbook

# Get Ready to Start Air Frying!

We've prepared this book for you so that you can enjoy everything about the air fryer you have in your kitchen. We made it really easy to navigate through this booklet and to help you out, we added measuring conversion chart at the end of this publication so you can take the guessing out of the equation. Also look in the back for out Bonus Marinade section for you to get creative with the meats and vegetables that you will be preparing for yourself, family and friends! Now turn the page and enjoy!

By Alicia Patterson

# Beef

Air Fryer Accessories Recipe Cookbook

# Beef Stir Fry

Prep Time: 30 Minutes / Cook Time: 13 Minutes / Servings: 4

## INGREDIENTS FOR MAKING THIS RECIPE:

1 pound of beef sirloin, cut into 2-inch strips
1½ pounds of broccoli florets
1 red pepper, cut into strips
1 green pepper, cut into strips
1 yellow pepper, cut into strips
½ cup of onion, cut into strips
½ cup of red onion, cut into strips
1 tablespoon stir fry oil
2 cups cooked rice of your choice

Sauce:
¼ cup of hoisin sauce
2 teaspoons of minced garlic
1 teaspoon of sesame oil
1 tablespoon of soy sauce
1 teaspoon of ground ginger
¼ cup of water

## DIRECTIONS FOR PREPARING THIS RECIPE:

- Mix all the sauce ingredients together in a bowl. Add in the beef and toss it until it's well coated. Cover the bowl and refrigerate for 20 minutes.
- While the beef is marinating, preheat your air fryer to 200F.
- Toss the vegetables with the stir fry oil.
- Place the vegetables in your preheated air fryer and allow them to cook for 5 minutes, until soft. If the vegetable is still somewhat firm cook them for 2 additional minutes.
- Set the cooked vegetables aside in a bowl.
- Raise the temperature on your air fryer to 360F. Add in the meat when it's done marinating. Allow the beef to cook for 4 minutes. If the beef isn't cooked to your liking flip it over and cook for 2 more minutes.
- Place the rice in 4 bowls and top it with the beef and vegetables.

By Alicia Patterson

# Beef Taco Eggrolls

Prep Time: 15 Minutes / Cook Time: 25 Minutes / Servings: 4
Use the Steel Metal Holder

## INGREDIENTS FOR MAKING THIS RECIPE:

*1 pound 90% lean ground beef*
*16 egg roll wrappers*
*1/2 onion chopped*
*1 can Cilantro Lime Rotel*
*1/2 can fat-free refried black beans*
*1/2 packet Taco Seasoning*
*1 cup reduced-fat shredded Mexican Cheese*
*1/2 cup whole kernel corn*
*1 tablespoon olive oil*
*2 garlic cloves, chopped*
*salt and pepper to taste*
*1 teaspoon chopped cilantro, optional*
*Cooking spray*

## DIRECTIONS FOR PREPARING THIS RECIPE:

- Preheat your air fryer to 400F.
- Use cooking spray to coat a skillet and heat the skillet on medium-high heat. Put In the onions and garlic, and allow them to cook until they become fragrant, a couple of minutes at most.
- Put in the beef, taco seasoning, salt and pepper, and allow the mixture to cook until the beef has browned. Make sure you break the meat up into small pieces while you cook it.
- Add in the corn, cilantro lime Rotel, and beans. Stir the mixture until it's well combined and then take it off the heat.
- You want to double wrap the eggrolls. Place the mixture in the middle of 8 doubled eggroll wrappers top the mixture with cheese. Use water to make the edges of the wrapper lightly moist. Use moisten edges to fold the sides of the egg roll towards the middle. Roll it up tightly. Complete the same process with the other wrappers.
- Brush the eggrolls with a light coating of olive oil and place half of them in your air fryer, put in the holder, and add the remaining eggrolls. Allow the eggrolls to cook for 8 minutes and then flip them over. Cook the eggrolls for 4 more minutes.
- Top the cooked eggrolls with cilantro and serve.

Air Fryer Accessories Recipe Cookbook

# Mongolian Beef with Green Beans

Prep Time: 20 Minutes / Cook Time: 20 Minutes / Servings: 4

## INGREDIENTS FOR MAKING THIS RECIPE:

*Meat:*
*1 Pound Flank Steak, thinly slice in long chunks*
*1/4 Cup Corn Starch*

*Sauce:*
*2 Teaspoon Vegetable Oil*
*1/2 Teaspoon Ginger*
*1 Tablespoon Minced Garlic*
*1/2 Cup Soy Sauce or Gluten Free Soy Sauce*
*1/2 Cup Water*
*3/4 Cup Brown Sugar, Packed*

*2 cups Cooked Rice*
*1 cup Cooked Green Beans*
*Green Onions, chopped*

## DIRECTIONS FOR PREPARING THIS RECIPE:

- Preheat your air fryer to 390F.
- Place the beef in your air fryer and cook it for 10 minutes and then flip it and cook for an additional 10 minutes.
- While the beef is cooking, heat a medium sauce pan on medium-high heat. Add in all the sauce ingredients and whisk them until the mixture comes to a low boil. Take the sauce off the heat.
- Put the cooked beef in a bowl and pour in the sauce. Allow the mixture to rest for about 10 minutes.
- While the beef is marinating place the cooked rice in 4 bowls and add top with the green beans.
- Remove the beef from the sauce and place it on top of rice. Sprinkle a little green onion on top. Drizzle on a little sauce if you'd like.
- Serve immediately.

By Alicia Patterson

# Beef Fried Rice

Prep Time: 10 Minutes / Cook Time: 20 Minutes / Servings: 6

## INGREDIENTS FOR MAKING THIS RECIPE:

*3 cups white rice cold, cooked*
*1 cup frozen peas and carrots*
*6 tbsps. soy sauce*
*1 tbsp. vegetable oil*
*1/2 cup onion diced*
*1 cup beef*
*Cooking spray*

## DIRECTIONS FOR PREPARING THIS RECIPE:

- Preheat your air fryer to 360F.
- Put the rice in a bowl and mix in the oil and soy sauce. Make sure all ingredients are well mixed.
- Mix in the onions, beef, peas and carrots. Make sure all ingredients are well mixed again.
- Put the mixture in a non-stick pan that's small enough to fit in your air fryer if you have one. If not spray cooking in a pan smaller enough to fit in your air fryer before adding in the mixture.
- Put the pan into your air fryer and allow it cook for 20 minutes.
- Once it's cooked, place the rice in a bowl or on a plate to serve.

Air Fryer Accessories Recipe Cookbook

# Beef Meatballs

Prep Time: 10 Minutes / Cook Time: 20 Minutes / Servings: 2 dozen meatballs
Use the Steel Metal Holder

## INGREDIENTS FOR MAKING THIS RECIPE:

*2 lbs. of ground beef*
*2 large eggs*
*1-1/4 cup bread crumbs*
*1/4 cup chopped fresh parsley*
*1 tsp. dried oregano*
*1/4 cup grated parmigiano reggiano*
*1 small clove garlic chopped*
*salt and pepper to taste*
*Cooking spray*

## DIRECTIONS FOR PREPARING THIS RECIPE:

- Spray the basket of your air fryer and steel metal holder with cooking spray.
- Preheat your air fryer to 350F.
- Mix together all the ingredients except for the cooking spray in a bowl, until well mixed.
- Use your hands to make 2-inch round balls out of the mixture.
- Place half the meatballs in your air fryer and then put in the steel metal holder and place the remaining meatballs on it. Cook for about 10-13 minutes. The meatballs should have a nice brown coloring. Flip them and cook for an additional 4-5 minutes.
- Place the cooked meatballs in some pasta sauce to absorb the flavor or serve them with your favorite pasta.

By Alicia Patterson

# Carne Asada Tacos

Prep Time: 3 Hours 15 Minutes / Cook Time: 20 Minutes / Servings:

## INGREDIENTS FOR MAKING THIS RECIPE:

*2 pounds Skirt Steak 1/2 thick or more*
*1 large Yellow Onion thinly sliced*
*Your favorite taco condiments*
*salsa*
*Corn or flour tortilla*

*Marinade:*
*4-5 whole Chipotle Peppers in Adobo from a can*
*2 roasted Pasilla Peppers*
*1/2 cup Freshly Squeezed Orange Juice*
*1/4 cup Freshly Squeezed Lime Juice*
*1/4 cup Freshly Squeeze Lemon Juice*
*6 cloves Fresh Garlic*
*2 Tablespoons Extra Virgin Olive Oil*
*1 cup Fresh Cilantro Leaves*
*2 Tablespoons Light Brown Sugar*
*1 Tablespoon Kosher Salt*
*2 teaspoons Ground Cumin*
*2 teaspoons Dried Oregano*
*1 teaspoon Freshly Ground Black Pepper*

## DIRECTIONS FOR PREPARING THIS RECIPE:

* Put all the marinade ingredient in a food processor or blender and blend until smooth. Save a ½ cup of the mixture if you'd like to use it for salsa.
* Place the onion and beef in either a bowl, dish, or re-sealable plastic bag and pour in the marinade. Allow the mixture to marinate, covered, in the refrigerator for at least 3 hours.
* Preheat your air fryer to 400F.
* Put the steak and onions in your air fryer and allow it to cook for 7-10 minute flipping after about 4 minutes if you want your meat medium. Adjust the cooking time up or down a couple of minutes for your desired doneness.
* Allow the steak to rest for about 5 minutes before slicing it thinly against the grain.
* Place the sliced carne asada in tacos along with your favorite condiments.

Air Fryer Accessories Recipe Cookbook

# Chicken Fried Steak

Prep Time: 20 Minutes / Cook Time: 20 Minutes / Servings: 1

## INGREDIENTS FOR MAKING THIS RECIPE:

*6 ounce sirloin steak-pounded thin*
*3 eggs, beaten*
*1 cup flour*
*1 cup Panko*
*1 teaspoon onion powder*
*1 teaspoon Garlic powder*
*1 teaspoon salt*
*1 teaspoon pepper*

*Gravy:*
*6 ounce ground sausage meat*
*2 tablespoon flour*
*2 cup milk*
*1 teaspoon pepper*

## DIRECTIONS FOR PREPARING THIS RECIPE:

- Preheat your air fryer to 370F.
- Mix the panko, onion and garlic powder, salt, and pepper together in a bowl.
- Place the flour in a bowl, and the eggs in another bowl.
- Coat the steak with flour, then egg, and finally the panko.
- Place the steak in your air fryer and cook it for 12 minutes
- While the steak is cooking, heat a medium pan on medium heat. Add in the sausage and cook until the sausage is completely cooked. Keep 2 tablespoons of the fat in the pan and remove the rest.
- Mix in the flour and once the ingredients are well mixed slowly stir in the milk.
- Allow the mixture to cook until the milk thickens. Season with the pepper. Cook for another 3 minutes to make sure the flour has fully incorporated.
- When the steak is cooked put it on a plate and top it with the gravy to serve.

By Alicia Patterson

# Beef Stuffed Roasted Bell Peppers

Prep Time: 20 Minutes / Cook Time: 20 Minutes / Servings: 2

## INGREDIENTS FOR MAKING THIS RECIPE:

*2 medium green peppers, stems and seeds removed*
*½ medium onion, chopped*
*1 clove garlic, minced*
*1 teaspoon olive oil*
*8 ounces lean ground beef*
*½ cup tomato sauce*
*1 teaspoon Worcestershire sauce*
*½ teaspoon salt*
*½ teaspoon black pepper*
*4 ounces cheddar cheese, shredded*

## DIRECTIONS FOR PREPARING THIS RECIPE:

- Put enough water in a medium size pot to cover the bell peppers. Salt the water to your taste and bring it to a boil. Once boiling add in the bell peppers and cook for 3 minutes.
- Pat the cooked bell peppers dry with paper towels.
- Place the olive oil in a small pan and heat on medium heat. Add in the onions and garlic and cook until the onions are brown, about 5-7 minutes. Take the mixture of the heat and let it cool.
- Preheat your air fryer to 390F.
- In a large bowl, mix together the Worcestershire sauce, garlic, onions, beef, half of the tomato sauce, salt, pepper, and half the cheese.
- Stuff each pepper with half the mixture and top with the left of tomato sauce and cheese.
- Place the peppers in your air fryer and cook for 15-20 minutes, until the beef is completely cooked.
- Serve immediately.

Air Fryer Accessories Recipe Cookbook

# Mini Meatloaf

Prep Time: 15 Minutes / Cook Time: 20 Minutes / Servings: 2

## INGREDIENTS FOR MAKING THIS RECIPE:

*Meatloaf:*
*1 pound 90% lean ground beef*
*½ medium onion, chopped*
*1/3 cup Kellog's corn flakes crumbs*
*1-2 tsps. salt*
*1-2 tsps. freshly ground black pepper*
*1 tsp (or 2 cloves) minced garlic*
*6 ounces tomato sauce*
*1 tsp dried basil*

*Glaze:*
*5 Tbsps. Heinz reduced-sugar ketchup*
*3 tsps. Splenda or Truvia brown sugar blend*
*1 tbsp. Worcestershire sauce*

*2 mini loaf pans*
*½ tbsp. lightly dried or fresh chopped Parsley*
*Cooking spray*

## DIRECTIONS FOR PREPARING THIS RECIPE:

- Preheat your air fryer to 390F.
- Mix together all of the meatloaf ingredients in a bowl, until well combined.
- Spray the inside of the mini loaf pans with cooking spray.
- Split the meatloaf mixture between 2 mini loaf pans.
- Place the glaze ingredients in a bowl and mix them together.
- Brush a nice coating of the glaze on the sides and top of the loaves.
- Put the loaves in your air fryer for 20 minutes.
- Brush the loaves again with the glaze at the 10 and 16 minute marks.
- Top the cooked loaves with parsley. Allow them to rest for a couple min.
- Remove the loaves from the pans and serve immediately.

By Alicia Patterson

# BBQ Bourbon Bacon Burger

Prep Time: 20 Minutes / Cook Time: 30 Minutes / Servings: 2

## INGREDIENTS FOR MAKING THIS RECIPE:

*Bacon:*
*1 tablespoon bourbon*
*2 tablespoons brown sugar*
*3 strips maple bacon, cut in half*

*Burger Patties:*
*¾ pound 80% lean ground beef*
*1 tablespoon minced onion*
*2 tablespoons BBQ sauce*
*½ teaspoon salt*
*freshly ground black pepper*

*Sauce:*
*2 tablespoons BBQ sauce*
*2 tablespoons mayonnaise*
*¼ teaspoon ground paprika*
*freshly ground black pepper*

*2 slices Colby Jack cheese or*
 *Monterey Jack*
*2 Kaiser rolls*
*lettuce and tomato for serving*

## DIRECTIONS FOR PREPARING THIS RECIPE:

- Preheat your air fryer to 390F.
- Mix together the brown sugar and bourbon. Brush, it on one side of the bacon.
- Place the bacon in your air fryer with the brushed side up and cook for 4 minutes. Flip the bacon over and brush the other side with the brown sugar mixture. Allow it to cook for 4 more minutes.
- During the cooking process, Mix the burger ingredients in a bowl until well combined. Make the mixture into 2 patties using your hands.
- When the bacon is done reduce the temperature 370F and put the beef patties in. Cook the burgers for 15 minutes if you like them rare and up to 20 minutes if you like them well done. Make sure the burger is flipped about halfway through the cooking process
- While the patties are cooking, mix together the sauce ingredients in a bowl adding salt and pepper to taste.
- When the burgers are cooked to your desired doneness put a piece of cheese on top and allow them to cook for 1 more minute.
- Spread a nice layer of sauce on the inside of your buns and place the patties with melted cheese in the middle with your desired condiments.
- Serve immediately with the side of your choice.

Air Fryer Accessories Recipe Cookbook

# Chicken

By Alicia Patterson

# Chicken Parm

Prep Time: 15 Minutes / Cook Time: 18 Minutes / Servings: 4
Use the Steel Metal Holder

## INGREDIENTS FOR MAKING THIS RECIPE:

2, 8 oz. chicken breast, sliced in half
6 tbsps. seasoned breadcrumbs
2 tbsps. grated Parmesan cheese
1 tbsp. butter, melted or olive oil
6 tbsps. mozzarella cheese
1/2 cup marinara
cooking spray

## DIRECTIONS FOR PREPARING THIS RECIPE:

- Spray the basket of your air fryer with cooking spray and metal holder. Preheat to 390F for at least 9 minutes.
- While the air fryer is preheating, mix together the bread crumbs and parmesan. Place the melted butter or olive oil in a separate bowl.
- Brush the chicken with a light coat of the olive oil or butter. Then dredge the chicken in the parmesan breadcrumb mixture.
- Place 2 pieces of chicken in the basket of the preheated air fryer. Spray a little cooking spray on top of the basket. Then put in the holder and add the remaining chicken.
- Cook the chicken pieces for 6 minutes and then flip them. Top the chicken with 1 tablespoon sauce and 1 ½ tablespoon cheese. Cook for about 3 more minutes, until the cheese melts.

Air Fryer Accessories Recipe Cookbook

# Honey Sriracha Hot Wings

Prep Time: 15 Minutes / Cook Time: 18 Minutes / Servings: 2

## INGREDIENTS FOR MAKING THIS RECIPE:

*1 pound chicken wings, tips removed and wings cut into individual drummettes and flats.*
*1/4 cup honey*
*2 tablespoons Sriracha sauce*
*1 1/2 tablespoons soy sauce*
*1 tablespoon butter*
*juice of 1/2 a lime*
*cilantro, chives, or scallions for garnish*

## DIRECTIONS FOR PREPARING THIS RECIPE:

- Preheat your air fryer to 360F.
- Once the air fryer is preheated, cook the chicken wings in the basket for 30 minutes. Flip the wings every 7 minutes to ensure they cook evenly.
- While the wings are cooking, mix the honey, Sriracha, soy, butter, and lime juice in a sauce pan and bring them to a boil. Allow them to boil for 3 minutes and then take them off the heat.
- Toss the cooked wings in the sauce. Top with garnish and serve immediately.

By Alicia Patterson

# Tandoori Chicken

Prep Time: 12 Hours 20 Minutes / Cook Time: 20 Minutes / Servings: 4
Use the Steel Metal Holder

## INGREDIENTS FOR MAKING THIS RECIPE:
*4 Chicken legs with thigh*

*Marinade 1:*
*3 tsps. Ginger paste*
*3 tsps. Garlic paste*
*Salt to taste*
*3 tbsps. Lemon juice*

*Marinade 2:*
*2 tbsps. Tandoori masala powder*
*1 tsp Roasted cumin powder*
*1 tsp Garam masala powder*
*2 tsps. Red chili powder*
*1 tsp Turmeric powder*
*4 tbsps. Hung curd -*
*2 tsps. Kasuri Methi*
*1 tsp Black pepper powder*
*2 tsps. Coriander powder*

## DIRECTIONS FOR PREPARING THIS RECIPE:
- Use a sharp knife to cut slits in the chicken.
- Mix all the ingredients together for marinade one in a bowl and add in the chicken.
- Cover the bowl and allow it to marinate for 15 minutes
- Mix together the ingredients for marinade 2 and pour it into the bowl with the chicken.
- Mix everything together until well combined.
- Cover the bowl and allow it to marinate in the refrigerator for 12-24 hours
- Use aluminum foil to line the basket of your air fryer.
- Preheat your air fryer to 290F.
- Add in half the chicken, put in the holder and  add the rest of the chicken, let it cook for 18-20 minutes. The chicken should be browned and lightly charred.

Air Fryer Accessories Recipe Cookbook

# Parmesan Garlic Chicken Wings

Prep Time: 5 Minutes / Cook Time: 24 Minutes / Servings: 4

## INGREDIENTS FOR MAKING THIS RECIPE:

*2 pounds wings + drumettes*
*3/4 cup grated parmesan cheese*
*2 tsps. minced garlic*
*2 tsps. fresh parsley, chopped*
*1 tsp salt*
*1 tsp pepper*
*Cooking spray*

## DIRECTIONS FOR PREPARING THIS RECIPE:

- Spray the basket of your air fryer with cooking spray.
- Preheat your air fryer at 400F for 4 minutes.
- Use a paper towel to pat the chicken wings dry.
- Combine the parmesan, garlic, salt, pepper, and parsley in a bowl. Make sure they're well mixed.
- Place the chicken wings in the bowl with the seasoning and toss until the chicken wings are well coated.
- Put the chicken wings in the air fryer and allow them to cook for 12 minutes before flipping them and allowing them to cook for about another 12 minutes. Check on the wings during the last few minutes to make sure they don't burn.
- Top the cooked wings with a little more parmesan and a few pieces of parsley as a garnish. Serve immediately.

By Alicia Patterson

# Parmesan Garlic Chicken Tenders

Prep Time: 5 Minutes / Cook Time: 12 Minutes / Servings: 4

## INGREDIENTS FOR MAKING THIS RECIPE:

*8 raw chicken tenders*
*1 egg*
*2 tablespoons of water*
*cooking spray*
*Dipping sauce of your choice*

*The Parmesan Garlic Coating:*
*1 cup panko breadcrumbs*
*1/2 tsp salt*
*1/4 tsp ground black pepper, or more to taste*
*1 tsp garlic powder*
*1/2 tsp onion powder*
*1/4 cup parmesan cheese*

## DIRECTIONS FOR PREPARING THIS RECIPE:

- Spray the basket of your air fryer with cooking spray.
- Preheat your air fryer to 400F.
- Mix together the parmesan garlic coating ingredients in a large bowl.
- Whisk together the water and egg in a medium bowl.
- Dip the chicken in the egg bowl and then in the parmesan bowl. Make sure the chicken is well coated.
- Place the chicken in your air fryer and cook for 12 minutes, flipping halfway through.
- Serve with your favorite dipping sauce.

Air Fryer Accessories Recipe Cookbook

# Pizza Stuffed Chicken Thighs

Prep Time: 10 Minutes / Cook Time: 15 Minutes / Servings: 3

## INGREDIENTS FOR MAKING THIS RECIPE:

*5 boneless, skinless, chicken thighs*
*½ cup pizza sauce*
*15 slices turkey pepperoni*
*½ small red onion, sliced*
*5 oz. sliced mozzarella cheese*
*½ cup shredded cheese for topping*

## DIRECTIONS FOR PREPARING THIS RECIPE:

- Preheat your air fryer at 370F.
- Spray the basket of your air fryer with cooking spray.
- Put the chicken thighs in the middle of 2 pieces of parchment paper. Pound the chicken until it thins out.
- Spread the pizza sauce on one side of the chicken then top it with 3 pieces of pepperoni and a couple pieces of onion.
- Place a slice of cheese on top of the pizza sauce, onion, and pepperoni.
- Fold the chicken over and use a toothpick to secure it shut.
- Cook the chicken thighs for 6 minutes and then flip for another 6 minutes. Place another piece of cheese on top of the thighs and cook for an additional 3 minutes.
- Remove the toothpicks and serve immediately.

By Alicia Patterson

# Thai Chicken Eggrolls

Prep Time: 10 Minutes / Cook Time: 8 Minutes / Servings: 4

Use the Steel Metal Holder

## INGREDIENTS FOR MAKING THIS RECIPE:

*4 egg roll wrappers*
*2 c. rotisserie chicken, shredded*
*¼ c. Thai peanut sauce*
*1 medium carrot, very thinly sliced or ribboned*
*3 green onions, chopped*
*¼ red bell pepper, julienned*
*non-stick cooking spray or sesame oil*

*Thai Peanut Sauce:*
*¾ c. light coconut milk*
*½ c. peanut butter*
*2 Tbsp. sesame oil*
*¼ c. fresh lime juice*
*2 Tbsp. soy sauce*
*3-4 Thai chili peppers, seeded, deveined & chopped or 1½ tsps. crushed red pepper flakes*
*1 Tbsp. rice wine vinegar*
*1 Tbsp. honey*
*¼ tsp. ground ginger*

## DIRECTIONS FOR PREPARING THIS RECIPE:

- Preheat your air fryer to 390F.
- Place the egg roll wrappers flat on a dry, clean surface.
- Put ¼ of all the vegetables on the bottom 3rd of one egg roll wrappers. Top the vegetables with a quarter of the chicken.
- Use water to make the edges of the wrapper lightly moist. Use the moisten edges to fold the sides of the egg roll towards the middle. Roll it up tightly. Complete the same process with the other wrappers. Make sure you keep the finished egg rolls under a damp paper towel.
- Coat the egg rolls with cooking spray on all sides.
- Put half the eggrolls in the basket, put in the holder, and put in the remaining eggrolls.
- Cook the egg rolls for about 6-8 minutes. The egg rolls will turn a nice golden brown and become crispy when done.
- Serve with a side of the peanut sauce.

Air Fryer Accessories Recipe Cookbook

# Chicken Nuggets

Prep Time: 12 Minutes / Cook Time: 8 Minutes / Servings: 4

## INGREDIENTS FOR MAKING THIS RECIPE:

*16 ounces skinless boneless chicken breasts, cut into 1-inch pieces*
*½ teaspoon kosher salt and black pepper, or more to taste*
*2 teaspoons olive oil*
*6 tablespoons whole wheat Italian seasoned breadcrumbs*
*2 tablespoons panko*
*2 tablespoons grated parmesan cheese*
*olive oil spray*
*your favorite dipping sauce*

## DIRECTIONS FOR PREPARING THIS RECIPE:

- Preheat your air fryer to 400F.
- Salt and pepper both sides of the chicken to taste.
- Mix the cheese, panko, and breadcrumbs in a bowl. Spray olive oil in another bowl.
- Put the chicken in the bowl with olive oil and cut the chicken with the olive oil.
- Then place the chicken in the other bowl and coat it with the mixture.
- Put the nuggets in your air fryer and spray the top with a little olive oil spray. Cook the nuggets for 8 minutes, making sure to flip them after 4 minutes. The nuggets will be golden brown when ready.
- Serve with dipping sauce of your choice.

By Alicia Patterson

# Roast Chicken

Prep Time: 10 Minutes / Cook Time: 1 Hour / Servings: 4-6

## INGREDIENTS FOR MAKING THIS RECIPE:

*1 whole chicken, 4 to 5 pounds*
*2 tsps. Mrs. Dash*
*2 tsps. sea salt*
*1 tsp garlic powder*
*1 tsp smoked paprika*
*1 tsp dry mustard*
*½ tsp black pepper*

## DIRECTIONS FOR PREPARING THIS RECIPE:

- Preheat your air fryer to 350F.
- Rinse the chicken and pat it dry.
- Mix all the ingredients except for the chicken in a bowl.
- Rub the spice mixture all over the chicken.
- Put the chicken your air fryer with the breast side down and cook it for 30 minutes.
- Flip the chicken over and cook it for an additional 30 minutes.
- Allow the chicken to rest for 10 minutes before you cut into it.

Air Fryer Accessories Recipe Cookbook

# Classic Fried Chicken Thighs

Prep Time: 5 Minutes / Cook Time: 25 Minutes / Servings: 4
Use the Steel Metal Holder

## INGREDIENTS FOR MAKING THIS RECIPE:

*1/2 cup all-purpose flour*
*1 egg beaten*
*4 small chicken thighs*
*1 1/2 tbsps. Old Bay Cajun Seasoning*
*1 tsp seasoning salt*

## DIRECTIONS FOR PREPARING THIS RECIPE:

- Preheat your air fryer to 390F.
- Place the flour, Cajun seasoning, and salt in a bowl and mix it together using a whisk.
- Coat the chicken with the seasoning mixture. Then dip it in the beaten egg. Then coat it with more of the seasoning mixture. Remove any extra flour.
- Put half the chicken in your air fryer, then put in the holder, put the rest of the chicken on it, and cook it for about 25 minutes.
- Serve immediately.

By Alicia Patterson

# Nashville Hot Fried Chicken

Prep Time: 5 Minutes / Cook Time: 25 Minutes / Servings: 4
Use the Steel Metal Holder

## INGREDIENTS FOR MAKING THIS RECIPE:

*1, 4-pound chicken, cut into 6 pieces, 2 breasts, 2 thighs and 2 drumsticks*
*2 eggs*
*1 cup buttermilk*
*2 cups all-purpose flour*
*2 tablespoons paprika*
*1 teaspoon garlic powder*
*1 teaspoon onion powder*
*2 teaspoons salt*
*1 teaspoon freshly ground black pepper*
*vegetable oil*

*Hot Sauce:*
*1 tablespoon cayenne pepper*
*1 teaspoon salt*
*¼ cup vegetable oil*

*4 slices white bread*
*dill pickle slices*
*cooking spray*

## DIRECTIONS FOR PREPARING THIS RECIPE:

- Spray the basket of your air fryer and the steel metal holder with cooking spray.
- Preheat your air fryer to 370F.
- Place the buttermilk and eggs in a bowl and whisk them together. Put the paprika, garlic and onion powder, salt, black pepper, and flour in a larger re-sealable plastic bag. Dip the chicken in the egg mixture and place it in the bag with seasoning. Seal the bag and shake it to coat the chicken. Repeat the process a second time.
- Spray a small amount of vegetable oil on the chicken.
- Place half the chicken in your air fryer and then place the steel metal holder in your air fryer. Place the remaining chicken on the steel metal holder.
- Cook the chicken for 20 minutes, making sure to flip the chicken after 10 minutes. Reduce the air fryer temperature to 340F and flip the chicken again. Cook for an additional 7 minutes.
- Towards the end of the cooking process, put the ¼ cup of oil in a small sauce pan and heat it on medium-high heat. Once the oil is hot, add in the remaining hot sauce ingredient and whisk everything together until it becomes a smooth sauce. Be careful because the seasoning will sizzle when it hits the hot oil.
- Put the white bread on a plate and place the chicken on top of it. Use a brush to the chicken with hot sauce. Top the chicken with pickles and serve.

Air Fryer Accessories Recipe Cookbook

# Honey Garlic Chicken Wings

Prep Time: 10 Minutes / Cook Time: 35 Minutes / Servings: 2

## INGREDIENTS FOR MAKING THIS RECIPE:

*16 Pieces Chicken Wings*
*3/4 cup Potato Starch*
*1/4 cup Clover Honey*
*1/4 cup Butter*
*4 Tablespoons Fresh Garlic minced*
*1/2 teaspoon Kosher Salt*
*1/8 cup Fresh Water or more as needed*
*cooking spray*

## DIRECTIONS FOR PREPARING THIS RECIPE:

- Spray the basket of your air fryer with cooking spray.
- Preheat your air fryer to 380 F.
- Wash and pat the chicken wings dry. Put the wings in a bowl and pour in the potato starch. Toss the chicken with the potato starch until well coated.
- Put the chicken wings in your air fryer and cook for 25 minutes. Make sure you shake the basket in 5 minute intervals.
- Raise the temperature to 400F and cook for an additional 5-10 minutes, until the wings are brown and completely dry.
- While the wings are cooking, heat up a small sauce pan over low heat. Once warm, put in the butter and allow it to melt, then mix in the oil. Add in the garlic and allow it to cook for 5 minutes.
- Pour in the salt and honey and allow the mixture to simmer for 20 minutes, making sure you stir it occasionally. Pour in a little water to stop the mixture from hardening at the 15-minute mark.
- Put the cooked wings on a plate or in a bowl and pour the sauce on top.

By Alicia Patterson

# Crispy Restaurant Style Chicken Sandwiches

Prep Time: 10 Minutes / Cook Time: 16 Minutes / Servings: 4

## INGREDIENTS FOR MAKING THIS RECIPE:

2 Boneless, Skinless Chicken
Breasts, pounded
1/2 cup Dill Pickle Juice
2 Eggs
1/2 cup Milk
1 cup All Purpose Flour
2 Tablespoons Powdered Sugar
1 teaspoon Paprika
1 teaspoon Sea Salt
1/2 teaspoon Freshly Ground Black
Pepper

1/2 teaspoon Garlic Powder
1/4 teaspoon Ground Celery
Seed ground
1 Tablespoon Extra Virgin Olive
Oil extra virgin
1 Oil Mister
4 Hamburger Buns toasted/buttered
8 Dill Pickle Chips or more
Cooking spray

## DIRECTIONS FOR PREPARING THIS RECIPE:

- Put the chicken in a re-sealable plastic bag, and pound the chicken until it's a ½ inch thick. Cut the pounded breasts in half.
- Put the chicken in another re-sealable plastic bag and add in the pickle juice. Seal the bag and shake it to coat the chicken. Allow it to marinate in the refrigerator for a minimum of 30 minutes.
- Spray the basket of your air fryer with cooking spray
- Preheat your air fryer to 340 F.
- Beat together the eggs and milk in a medium sized bowl. Place all the spices and flour in another medium bowl and mix them together.
- Dip the chicken in the egg mixture and then coat it with the spice mixture. Shake off any excess flour.
- Spray the chicken with oil and then put it in your air fryer. Allow the chicken to cook for 6 minutes. After 6 minutes spray the chicken with more oil and flip it. Cook for an additional 6 minutes. Increase the temperature to 400F and continue to cook the chicken for 4 minutes, flipping halfway through.
- Place the cooking chicken on hamburger buns and top with 2 pickles chips and a little mayonnaise.
- Serve immediately.

Air Fryer Accessories Recipe Cookbook

# BBQ Chicken

Prep Time: 15 Minutes / Cook Time: 25 Minutes / Servings: 4

## INGREDIENTS FOR MAKING THIS RECIPE:

*1, 3 ½ pound chicken, cut into 8 serving pieces*
*1 Tablespoon smoked paprika*
*2 tsps. kosher salt*
*1 tsp garlic powder*
*1/2 tsp freshly ground black pepper*
*1 tsp light brown sugar*
*1 1/2 BBQ Sauce of your choice, plus more for serving*

## DIRECTIONS FOR PREPARING THIS RECIPE:

- Preheat your air fryer to 375F.
- Mix all the spices together in a bowl.
- Rub every piece of chicken with the spices to mix.
- Put the chicken with the skin side down in your air fryer and cook it for 20 minutes.
- Take the chicken out reduce the temperature to 350F, and brush the chicken with BBQ sauce of your choice.
- Cook the chicken for 5-10 more minutes, until completely cooked.
- Serve chicken with a side of your favorite BBQ sauce.

By Alicia Patterson

# Spicy BBQ Chicken

Prep Time: 15 Minutes / Cook Time: 25 Minutes / Servings: 4

## INGREDIENTS FOR MAKING THIS RECIPE:

*1, 3 ½ pound chicken, cut into 8 serving pieces*
*1 Tablespoon smoked paprika*
*2 tsps. kosher salt*
*1 tsp garlic powder*
*1/2 tsp freshly ground black pepper*
*1/8 tsp cayenne pepper*
*1 tsp. oregano*
*1 tsp light brown sugar*
*1 1/2 BBQ Sauce of your choice, plus more for serving*

## DIRECTIONS FOR PREPARING THIS RECIPE:

- Preheat your air fryer to 375F.
- Mix all the spices together in a bowl.
- Rub every piece of chicken with the spicy mixture
- Put the chicken with the skin side down in your air fryer and cook it for 20 minutes.
- Take the chicken out reduce the temperature to 350F, and brush the chicken with BBQ sauce of your choice.
- Cook the chicken for 5-10 more minutes, until completely cooked.
- Serve chicken with a side of your favorite BBQ sauce.

Air Fryer Accessories Recipe Cookbook

# Crispy Chicken Breast

Prep Time: 10 Minutes / Cook Time: 10 Minutes / Servings: 4
Use the Steel Metal Holder

## INGREDIENTS FOR MAKING THIS RECIPE:

*1 pound boneless skinless chicken breasts*
*1 tablespoon olive oil*

*Breading:*
*¼ cup bread crumbs*
*½ teaspoon salt*
*¼ teaspoon black pepper*
*½ teaspoon paprika*
*1/8 teaspoon garlic powder*
*1/8 teaspoon onion powder*

## DIRECTIONS FOR PREPARING THIS RECIPE:

- Preheat your air fryer to 390F.
- Slice the chicken breasts in half. This will create 2 thin chicken breast that will cook quicker.
- Brush the breast with a coat of olive oil
- Mix all the breading ingredients together in a bowl. Dip the chicken breasts into the mixture until they're completely coated. Shake off any excess mixture from the chicken.
- Put half the chicken in your air fryer, put in the holder, add the remaining chicken, and allow them to cook for 4 minutes, then flip them and cook for 2 additional minutes. Check to see if the chicken is done and cook for a few additional minutes if necessary.

By Alicia Patterson

# Crispy Spicy Chicken Breast

Prep Time: 10 Minutes / Cook Time: 10 Minutes / Servings: 4

Use the Steel Metal Holder

## INGREDIENTS FOR MAKING THIS RECIPE:

*1 pound boneless skinless chicken breasts*
*1 tablespoon olive oil*

*Breading:*
*¼ cup bread crumbs*
*½ teaspoon salt*
*¼ teaspoon black pepper*
*½ teaspoon paprika*
*1/8 teaspoon garlic powder*
*1/8 teaspoon onion powder*
*¼ teaspoon cayenne pepper*

## DIRECTIONS FOR PREPARING THIS RECIPE:

- Preheat your air fryer to 390F.
- Slice the chicken breasts in half. This will create 2 thin chicken breast that will cook quicker.
- Brush the breast with a coat of olive oil
- Mix all the breading ingredients together in a bowl. Dip the chicken breasts into the mixture until they're completely coated. Shake off any excess mixture from the chicken.
- Put half the chicken in your air fryer, put in the holder, add the remaining chicken, and allow them to cook for 4 minutes, then flip them and cook for 2 additional minutes. Check to see if the chicken is done and cook for a few additional minutes if necessary.

Air Fryer Accessories Recipe Cookbook

# Jerk Chicken Wings

Prep Time: 2 hours 10 Minutes / Cook Time: 30 Minutes / Servings: 6
Use the Steel Metal Holder

## INGREDIENTS FOR MAKING THIS RECIPE:

3 pounds chicken wings
2 tablespoons olive oil
2 tablespoons soy sauce
6 cloves garlic, finely chopped
1 habanero pepper seeds and ribs removed finely chopped
1 tablespoon allspice
1 teaspoon cinnamon
1 teaspoon Cayenne pepper
1 teaspoon white pepper
1 teaspoon sea salt
2 tablespoons brown sugar
1 tablespoon fresh thyme, finely chopped
1 tablespoon fresh ginger, grated
4 scallions, finely chopped
5 tablespoons Lime Juice
1/2 cup Red wine vinegar
Ranch dressing or blue cheese dressing

## DIRECTIONS FOR PREPARING THIS RECIPE:

- Combine all ingredients in a large bowl or large re-sealable plastic bag. Add chicken and shake if you're using a bag or toss the chicken if using a bowl.
- Cover the bowl if using or place the sealed bag in your refrigerator for 2-24 hours to marinate.
- Preheat your air fryer to 390F.
- Take the wings out of the liquid and use a paper towel to pat them dry
- Place half the marinated chicken in your air fryer, then the holder, put in the remaining chicken and cook for 14-16 minutes. Make sure you shake the basket halfway through.
- Serve immediately with a side of blue cheese or ranch dressing,

By Alicia Patterson

# Bloody Mary Wings

Wings and alcohol are always a winning pair. The wings marinate in a delicious bloody mary sauce that includes vodka. The wings come out packed with all the boozy alcohol flavor you want.

Prep Time: 1 Hour 10 Minutes / Cook Time: 25 Minutes / Servings: 6

## INGREDIENTS FOR MAKING THIS RECIPE:

3 lbs. chicken wings
celery salt
Freshly ground black pepper

Dip:
2/3 c. sour cream
2 tsp. horseradish
2 tsp. chopped dill

Bloody Mary Sauce:
3 cups tomato juice
2/3 c. vodka
3/4 c. brown sugar
1/3 c. Hot sauce, such as Tabasco
1 tbsp. horseradish
1 tbsp. Worcestershire sauce
Juice of 1 lemon
kosher salt
Freshly ground black pepper

## DIRECTIONS FOR PREPARING THIS RECIPE:

- Rinse the chicken wings and use a paper towel to pat them dry.
- Season the dry wings with celery salt and pepper
- Mix together the bloody mary ingredients in a large bowl. Reserve about 1 ½ cups for later.
- Add the wings to the bowl of bloody mary sauce. Toss the wings and submerge them in the sauce. Add some of the reserved sauce if they aren't totally covered. Cover the bowl and place it in the refrigerator for at least 1 hour.
- Preheat your air fryer to 380F.
- Take the wings out of the bowl and pat the wings dry.
- Place the chicken wing in your air fryer and allow them to cook for 25, making sure to shake the basket at the halfway point.
- While the chicken wings are cooking, heat a medium sauce pan on medium heat and add the reserved bloody mary sauce. Let the sauce come to a simmer and then cover it. Let it continue cooking until it reduces by half.
- Place the dip ingredients in a bowl and use a whisk to combine them.
- Place the wings in a big bowl and pour the sauce over it. Toss the wings in the sauce until they're well coated.
- Serve immediately with a side of the dip.

Air Fryer Accessories Recipe Cookbook

# Buffalo Wings

Prep Time: 5 Minutes / Cook Time: 30 Minutes / Servings: 8

## INGREDIENTS FOR MAKING THIS RECIPE:

4 pounds Chicken Wing Sections
½ cup Frank's Red-Hot Cayenne Pepper Sauce
½ cup Butter
1 Tablespoon Worcestershire Sauce
1-2 Tablespoons Light Brown Sugar, optional
1 teaspoon Kosher Salt

## DIRECTIONS FOR PREPARING THIS RECIPE:

- Preheat your air fryer to 380F.
- Rinse the chicken wings and use a paper towel to pat them dry.
- Place the chicken wing in your air fryer and allow them to cook for 25, making sure to shake the basket at the halfway point.
- While the chicken wings are cooking, whisk together the remaining ingredients.
- After the 25 minutes shake the basket again, and raise the temperature to 400F. Allow the chicken to cook for 5 additional minutes.
- Place the wings in a big bowl and pour the sauce over it. Toss the wings in the sauce until they're well coated.
- Serve immediately.

By Alicia Patterson

# Delicious Honey Dijon Wings

Prep Time: 5 Minutes / Cook Time: 30 Minutes / Servings: 8

## INGREDIENTS FOR MAKING THIS RECIPE:

*4 pounds Chicken Wing Sections*
*½ cup Dijon Mustard*
*½ cup Butter*
*1 Honey*
*1-2 Tablespoons Light Brown Sugar, optional*
*1 teaspoon Kosher Salt*

## DIRECTIONS FOR PREPARING THIS RECIPE:

- Preheat your air fryer to 380F.
- Rinse the chicken wings and use a paper towel to pat them dry.
- Place the chicken wing in your air fryer. Lightly spray with oil and allow them to cook for 25 min. Shake the basket at the halfway point.
- While the chicken wings are cooking, whisk together the remaining ingredients.
- After the 25 minutes shake the basket again, and raise the temperature to 400F. Allow the chicken to cook for 5 additional minutes.
- Place the wings in a big bowl and pour the sauce over it. Toss the wings in the sauce until they're well coated.
- Serve immediately.

Air Fryer Accessories Recipe Cookbook

# Spicy Peach Chicken Wings

Prep Time: 10 Minutes / Cook Time: 30 Minutes / Servings: 6

## INGREDIENTS FOR MAKING THIS RECIPE:

*Kosher salt*
*1 teaspoon smoked paprika*
*1/2 teaspoon garlic powder*
*3 pounds chicken wings, cut at joint*
*1/2 stick (2 ounces) butter*
*2 cloves garlic, chopped*
*1/2 cup peach preserves*
*1/4 cup hot sauce, like Tabasco*
*1 tablespoon soy sauce*

## DIRECTIONS FOR PREPARING THIS RECIPE:

- Preheat your air fryer to 380F.
- Rinse the chicken wings and use a paper towel to pat them dry.
- Combine the garlic powder and paprika
- Coat the chicken wings with the seasoning mix.
- Place the chicken wing in your air fryer and allow them to cook for 25, making sure to shake the basket at the halfway point.
- While the chicken wings are cooking, heat a medium sauce pan on medium heat and melt the butter along with the garlic.
- Mix in the soy sauce, hot sauce, and peach preserve. Allow the mixture to cook for about 5 minutes, until it becomes thick and syrupy.
- After the 25 minutes shake the basket again, and raise the temperature to 400F. Allow the chicken to cook for 5 additional minutes.
-  Place the wings in a big bowl and pour the sauce over it. Toss the wings in the sauce until they're well coated.
- Serve immediately.

By Alicia Patterson

# Cilantro Lime Chicken Wings

Prep Time: 10 Minutes / Cook Time: 30 Minutes / Servings: 6

## INGREDIENTS FOR MAKING THIS RECIPE:

¼ cup extra-virgin olive oil
Juice of 2 limes
1 teaspoon garlic powder
1 teaspoon ground cumin
1/2 teaspoon smoked paprika
3 pounds chicken wings
kosher salt
Freshly ground black pepper

GLAZE:
4 tablespoons butter
2 tablespoons honey
1 tablespoon. Hot sauce
Juice of 1 lime
2 tablespoons Chopped cilantro

## DIRECTIONS FOR PREPARING THIS RECIPE:

- Preheat your air fryer to 380F.
- Rinse the chicken wings and use a paper towel to pat them dry.
- Put the paprika, lime juice, cumin, and garlic powder in a big bowl and use a whisk to mix them together. Place the chicken wings in the bowl and toss them in the mixture. Cover the bowl and allow the wings to marinate in the refrigerator for at least an hour.
- Take the wings out of the marinade and use a paper towel to pat them dry.
- Place the chicken wing in your air fryer and allow them to cook for 25, making sure to shake the basket at the halfway point.
- While the chicken wings are cooking, heat a small sauce pan on medium heat and melt the butter in it. Use a whisk to mix in the lime juice, hot sauce, and honey. Take the sauce off the heat and stir in the cilantro
- After the 25 minutes shake the basket again, and raise the temperature to 400F. Allow the chicken to cook for 5 additional minutes. Salt and pepper the wings to taste.
- Place the wings in a big bowl and pour the sauce over it. Toss the wings in the sauce until they're well coated.
- Serve immediately.

Air Fryer Accessories Recipe Cookbook

# Mongolian Chicken Wings

Prep Time: 10 Minutes / Cook Time: 33 Minutes / Servings: 3

## INGREDIENTS FOR MAKING THIS RECIPE:

*1 1/2 pounds chicken wings*
*kosher salt*
*Freshly ground black pepper*

*Sauce:*
*1/4 c. low-sodium soy sauce*
*1/4 c. honey*
*2 tbsp. rice wine vinegar*
*1 tbsp. Sriracha*
*3 cloves garlic, minced*
*1 tbsp. grated fresh ginger*

*Green onions, for garnish*
*Sesame seeds, for garnish*

## DIRECTIONS FOR PREPARING THIS RECIPE:

- Preheat your air fryer to 380F.
- Rinse the chicken wings and use a paper towel to pat them dry.
- Season the wings with salt and pepper to taste.
- Place the chicken wing in your air fryer and allow them to cook for 25, making sure to shake the basket at the halfway point.
- While the chicken wings are cooking, add the sauce ingredients to a medium sauce pan and bring the mixture to a simmer. Once the mixture is simmering lower the heat a little. Allow the mixture to cook for 10 minutes.
- After the 25 minutes shake the basket again, and raise the temperature to 400F. Allow the chicken to cook for 5 additional minutes.
- Preheat your broiler.
- Place the wings in a big bowl and pour the sauce over it. Toss the wings in the sauce until they're well coated. Place the coated wings on a baking sheet and place them under the broiler for 2-3 minutes, until the wings caramelize.

By Alicia Patterson

# Root Beer BBQ Wings

Prep Time: 10 Minutes / Cook Time: 33 Minutes / Servings: 6

## INGREDIENTS FOR MAKING THIS RECIPE:

*Sauce:*
*3/4 c. root beer*
*1 c. ketchup*
*1 tbsp. light brown sugar*
*2 tbsp. honey*
*1 tbsp. Worcestershire sauce*
*Juice of 1 lime*
*1/2 tsp. garlic powder*
*1/2 tsp. onion powder*

*3 lb. chicken wings*
*kosher salt*
*Freshly ground black pepper*

## DIRECTIONS FOR PREPARING THIS RECIPE:

- Preheat your air fryer to 380F.
- Rinse the chicken wings and use a paper towel to pat them dry.
- Season the wings with salt and pepper to taste.
- Place the chicken wing in your air fryer and allow them to cook for 25, making sure to shake the basket at the halfway point.
- While the chicken wings are cooking, add the sauce ingredients to a medium sauce pan, whisk them together, and heat on medium-low heat. Bring the mixture to a simmer. Once the mixture is simmering, allow the mixture to cook until it reduces a little, around 8-10 minutes.
- After the 25 minutes shake the basket again, and raise the temperature to 400F. Allow the chicken to cook for 5 additional minutes.
- Preheat your broiler.
- Place the wings in a big bowl and pour the sauce over it. Toss the wings in the sauce until they're well coated. Place the coated wings on a baking sheet and place them under the broiler for 2-3 minutes, until the wings caramelize.

Air Fryer Accessories Recipe Cookbook

# Balsamic Glazed Wings

Prep Time: 10 Minutes / Cook Time: 35 Minutes / Servings: 4

## INGREDIENTS FOR MAKING THIS RECIPE:

*Glaze:*
*Freshly ground black pepper*
*1 1/4 c. balsamic vinegar*
*2 tbsps. honey*
*3 cloves garlic, finely minced*

*2 pounds party chicken wings*
*1 tbsp. Italian seasoning*
*Salt and pepper*
*Caesar dressing, for dipping*

## DIRECTIONS FOR PREPARING THIS RECIPE:

- Preheat your air fryer to 380F.
- Rinse the chicken wings and use a paper towel to pat them dry.
- Season the wings with Italian seasoning, salt, and pepper to taste.
- Place the chicken wing in your air fryer and allow them to cook for 25, making sure to shake the basket at the halfway point.
- While the chicken wings are cooking, add the sauce ingredients to a medium sauce pan, whisk them together, and heat on medium-low heat. Bring the mixture to a simmer. Once the mixture is simmering, allow the mixture to cook until it reduces a little, around 8-10 minutes.
- After the 25 minutes shake the basket again, and raise the temperature to 400F. Allow the chicken to cook for 5 additional minutes.
- Preheat your broiler.
- Place the wings in a big bowl and pour the sauce over it. Toss the wings in the sauce until they're well coated. Place the coated wings on a baking sheet and place them under the broiler for5 minutes, until the wings caramelize.
- Serve immediately with a side of Caesar dressing if you'd like.

By Alicia Patterson

# Korean BBQ Wings

Prep Time: 10 Minutes / Cook Time: 35 Minutes / Servings: 3

## INGREDIENTS FOR MAKING THIS RECIPE:

*1 1/2 lb. chicken wingettes and drumettes*
*kosher salt*
*Freshly ground pepper*

*BBQ Sauce:*
*1/4 c. ketchup*
*1/4 c. Sriracha*
*2 tbsps. honey*
*1 tsp. lemon juice*

*Toasted sesame seeds, for garnishing*

## DIRECTIONS FOR PREPARING THIS RECIPE:

- Preheat your air fryer to 380F.
- Rinse the chicken wings and use a paper towel to pat them dry.
- Season the wings with salt, and pepper to taste.
- Place the chicken wing in your air fryer and allow them to cook for 25, making sure to shake the basket at the halfway point.
- While the chicken wings are cooking, add the sauce ingredients to a medium sized bowl, whisk them together, until the sauce becomes smooth.
- After the 25 minutes shake the basket again, and raise the temperature to 400F. Allow the chicken to cook for 5 additional minutes.
- Place the wings in the bowl with the sauce. Toss the wings in the sauce until they're well coated.
- Serve immediately with a garnish of sesame seeds.

Air Fryer Accessories Recipe Cookbook

# Jack Daniels BBQ Wings

Prep Time: 10 Minutes / Cook Time: 35 Minutes / Servings: 6

## INGREDIENTS FOR MAKING THIS RECIPE:

*3 pounds chicken wings, (split at the joints, tips removed)*
*kosher salt*
*Freshly ground black pepper*

*BBQ Sauce:*
*2 tbsps. extra-virgin olive oil*
*1/2 yellow onion, minced*
*2 1/2 cups ketchup*
*1/4 c. molasses*
*1/3 c. apple cider vinegar*
*1/4 c. packed brown sugar*
*2 tbsps. tomato paste*
*1/4 c. Worcestershire sauce*
*1/3 c. Jack Daniel's whiskey*

## DIRECTIONS FOR PREPARING THIS RECIPE:

- Preheat your air fryer to 380F.
- Rinse the chicken wings and use a paper towel to pat them dry.
- Season the wings with salt, and pepper to taste.
- Place the chicken wing in your air fryer and allow them to cook for 25, making sure to shake the basket at the halfway point.
- While the chicken wings are cooking, pour the olive oil in a medium sauce pan, and heat on medium heat. Put in the onions and cook until they become soft. Mix in the garlic and allow it to cook for 30 seconds, until it's fragrant. Then add in the remaining sauce ingredients and allow it to come to a simmer. Cook the simmering sauce for about 5-10 minutes, until it reduces a little and the flavors come together.
- After the 25 minutes shake the basket again, and raise the temperature to 400F. Allow the chicken to cook for 5 additional minutes.
- Place the wings in a bowl and pour in the sauce. Toss the wings in the sauce until they're well coated.

By Alicia Patterson

# Pork

Air Fryer Accessories Recipe Cookbook

# Breaded Pork Chops

Prep Time: 10 Minutes / Cook Time: 16 Minutes / Servings: 4
Use the Steel Metal Holder

## INGREDIENTS FOR MAKING THIS RECIPE:

*1/2 cup Dijon mustard*
*4 pork loin chops 3/4-inch thick*
*1 cup Italian bread crumbs*
*1/2 teaspoon salt*
*1/2 teaspoon black pepper*
*1/4 teaspoon cayenne pepper*
*1 teaspoon smoked paprika*
*Cooking spray*

## DIRECTIONS FOR PREPARING THIS RECIPE:

- Spray the basket of your air fryer with cooking spray.
- Preheat your air fryer to 390F.
- Spread a layer of the mustard all over the pork chops
- Place the bread crumbs and spices in a bowl and mix them together.
- Coat the pork chops with the bread crumb mixture.
- Place half the pork chops in your air fryer, put in the holder, add the remaining pork chops, and cook them for 8 minutes per side.
- Serve immediately with the side of your choice.

By Alicia Patterson

# Parmesan Crusted Pork Chops

Prep Time: 10 Minutes / Cook Time: 15 Minutes / Servings: 4
Use the Steel Metal Holder

## INGREDIENTS FOR MAKING THIS RECIPE:

4 thick center cut boneless pork chops
1/2 tsps. Salt
1/4 tsps. Pepper
1 tsps. Smoked Paprika
1/2 tsps. onion powder
1/4 tsps. chili powder
2 large eggs, beaten
1 cup pork rind crumbs
3 tablespoons grated parmesan cheese
Cooking spray

## DIRECTIONS FOR PREPARING THIS RECIPE:

- Spray the basket of your air fryer with cooking spray.
- Preheat your air fryer to 400F.
- Place the pork rinds in a blender or food processer and pulse until they become crumbs.
- Mix together the paprika, onion powder, chili powder, pork rind crumbs, salt, pepper, and parmesan in a bowl.
- Put the beaten eggs in a different bowl.
- Coat the pork chops with the eggs, and then coat it with the pork rind mixture.
- Place the pork chops in your air fryer, add in the holder, put in the remaining pork chops, and cook for 12-15 minutes flipping halfway through.

Air Fryer Accessories Recipe Cookbook

# Garlic Butter Pork Chops

Prep Time: 1 Hour 10 Minutes / Cook Time: 16 Minutes / Servings: 4
Use the Steel Metal Holder

## INGREDIENTS FOR MAKING THIS RECIPE:

*4 Pork Chops*
*1 tbsp. Coconut Butter*
*1 tbsp. Coconut Oil*
*2 tsps. Garlic Cloves grated*
*2 tsps. Parsley*
*Salt & Pepper*

## DIRECTIONS FOR PREPARING THIS RECIPE:

- Mix together all the ingredients in a bowl except for the pork chops.
- Coat the pork chops with the mixture and wrap the pork chops in aluminum foil.
- Place the wrapped pork chops in the refrigerator for an hour.
- Take the pork chops out of the aluminum foil and sprinkle with any seasoning that may have stuck to the aluminum foil.
- Put the pork chops in your air fryer and cook them for 7 minutes. Flip the pork chops and cook them for an additional 8 minutes.
- Serve immediately with the side of your choice.

By Alicia Patterson

# Bacon Wrapped Pork Tenderloin with Apples and Gravy

Prep Time: 15 Minutes / Cook Time: 30 Minutes / Servings: 4

## INGREDIENTS FOR MAKING THIS RECIPE:

1 Pork Tenderloin
3-4 strips of bacon
1-2 tablespoons Dijon mustard

Chopped rosemary or thyme for garnish
Cooking spray

**Apples with Gravy:**
2-3 Granny Smith apples, cut in cubes
or your favorite kind of apples
1 small onion or shallot, chopped
2 tablespoons butter, divided
1 tablespoons all-purpose flour
1 cup of vegetable broth
1/2 - 1 tsp. of Dijon mustard, optional
salt & pepper to taste

## DIRECTIONS FOR PREPARING THIS RECIPE:

- Spray the basket of your air fryer with cooking spray.
- Preheat your air fryer to 360F.
- Coat the pork tenderloin with the Dijon. Then wrap the bacon around the meat.
- Place the tenderloin in your air fryer and cook for 15 minutes. Flip it over and cook for an additional 10-15 minutes, until fully cooked.
- While the tenderloin is cooking, heat a medium sauce pan on medium heat and then add in 1 tablespoon of butter. Melt the butter and add in the shallots. Allow the shallots to cook for 1-2 minutes, until they soften.
- Mix in the apples and allow the mixture to cook for 3-5 more minutes, until the apples soften. Place the cooked mixture in a bowl and set it aside.
- Heat a small sauce pan on medium heat and add in the remaining butter and let it melt. Add in the flour and stir together until a paste begins to form
- Stir in the broth slowly allowing it to blend together with the flour. Mix in the mustard at this point if you're using it. Lower the heat to medium-low and cook, stirring occasionally, until the mixture starts to simmer, and bubbles start to pop up at the edges. Then pour in 1 cup of the apples. Let the mixture cook until it starts to thicken up.
- Allow the cooked pork to sit for 5 minutes before cutting it.
- Top the sliced pork with the apples and gravy.
- Garnish with thyme or rosemary and serve.

Air Fryer Accessories Recipe Cookbook

# Easy Pork Taquitos

Prep Time: 15 Minutes / Cook Time: 30 Minutes / Servings: 4
Use the Pizza Pan

## INGREDIENTS FOR MAKING THIS RECIPE:

30 oz. of cooked shredded pork tenderloin
2 1/2 cups shredded Mexican cheese blend
10 small flour tortillas
Juice of 1 lime
Cooking spray
Salsa for dipping, optional
Sour Cream, optional
Cooking spray

## DIRECTIONS FOR PREPARING THIS RECIPE:

- Preheat your air fryer to 380F.
- Pour the lime juice over the pork and mix it together so all the pork is evenly coated with the juice.
- Microwave the tortillas in 2 even batches for 10 seconds under a damp paper towel.
- Add an even amount of cheese and pork to the middle of each tortilla.
- Be gentle as you roll the tortillas tightly.
- Line the pizza pan with aluminum foil, spray it with cooking spray, and place the taquitos on it.
- Spray another coating of cooking spray on the taquitos.
- Place the pan in your air fryer and cook for 7-10 minutes, flipping halfway through.
- Serve the taquitos with a side of sour cream and salsa if you'd like.

By Alicia Patterson

# Bacon Wrapped Cajun Jalapeños

Prep Time: 8 Minutes / Cook Time: 15-18 Minutes / Servings: 4

## INGREDIENTS FOR MAKING THIS RECIPE:

*1 lb bacon, raw uncooked*
*1 large sweet onion, cut into wedges*
*6 fresh jalapeno peppers*
*2 teaspoons seafood seasoning, or*
*2 teaspoons cayenne pepper*

## DIRECTIONS FOR PREPARING THIS RECIPE:

- Preheat oven to 350 degrees F.
- Set shrimp aside in a bowl after peeled and washed. start an assembly line.
- Cut the bacon in half vertically then put on a plate.
- Cut and peel onion into wedges and separate, then put in a bowl.
- Wash the Jalapenos thoroughly, then slice into thirds long ways. Remove the seeds and place in a bowl.
- Start assembly with a shrimp, a slice of Jalapeno, and a slice of onion. Holding all in your hand, wrap bacon around and secure with a wooded toothpick. Repeat with each shrimp.
- Place on a baking sheet.
- Sprinkle with seasoning.
- Place in the oven and roast until bacon is slightly crisp. Roasting time may be adjusted.

Air Fryer Accessories Recipe Cookbook

# Bacon Wrapped Shrimp Jalapeños

Prep Time: 8 Minutes / Cook Time: 15-18 Minutes / Servings: 4

## INGREDIENTS FOR MAKING THIS RECIPE:

*1lb large shrimp, peeled and cleaned*
*1lb bacon, raw uncooked*
*1large sweet onion, cut into wedges*
*6fresh jalapeno peppers*
*2teaspoons seafood seasoning, or*
*2teaspoons cayenne pepper*

## DIRECTIONS FOR PREPARING THIS RECIPE:

- Preheat oven to 350 degrees F.
- Set shrimp aside in a bowl after peeled and washed. start an assembly line.
- Cut the bacon in half vertically then put on a plate.
- Cut and peel onion into wedges and separate, then put in a bowl.
- Wash the Jalapenos thoroughly, then slice into thirds long ways. Remove the seeds and place in a bowl.
- Start assembly with a shrimp, a slice of Jalapeno, and a slice of onion. Holding all in your hand, wrap bacon around and secure with a wooded toothpick. Repeat with each shrimp.
- Place on a baking sheet.
- Sprinkle with seasoning.
- Place in the oven and roast until bacon is slightly crisp. Roasting time may be adjusted.

By Alicia Patterson

# Seafood

Air Fryer Accessories Recipe Cookbook

# Spicy Crunchy Shrimp

Prep Time: 10 Minutes / Cook Time: 8 Minutes / Servings: 4
Use the Skewer Rack

## INGREDIENTS FOR MAKING THIS RECIPE:

*1 pound raw shrimp, peeled and deveined*
*1 egg white*
*1/2 cup all-purpose flour*
*3/4 cup panko bread crumbs*
*1 tsp paprika*
*Montreal Chicken Seasoning to taste*
*salt and pepper to taste*
*cooking spray*

## DIRECTIONS FOR PREPARING THIS RECIPE:

- Spray the basket of your air fryer and the metal skewer with cooking spray.
- Preheat your air fryer to 400F.
- Put the flour, egg whites, and panko into 3 separate bowls. Add the rest of the seasoning to the bowl with panko and mix until well combined.
- Dip the shrimp in the flour, then egg whites, then the panko mixture.
- Place the shrimp on the skewer rack and place it in your air fryer and cook them for 4 minutes per side.
- While the shrimp are cooking, mix together the spicy sauce ingredients in a bowl.
- Serve the cooked shrimp with a side of the spicy sauce.

By Alicia Patterson

# Cajun Shrimp

Prep Time: 10 Minutes / Cook Time: 16 Minutes / Servings: 2
Use the Skewer Rack

## INGREDIENTS FOR MAKING THIS RECIPE:

1/2 pound tiger shrimp 16-20 count
1/4 teaspoon cayenne pepper
1/2 teaspoon old bay seasoning
1/4 teaspoon smoked paprika
1 pinch of salt
1 tablespoon olive oil
Cooking spray

## DIRECTIONS FOR PREPARING THIS RECIPE:

- Spray the basket of your air fryer and skewer rack with cooking spray.
- Preheat your air fryer to 390F.
- Mix all the seasoning together in a bowl.
- Toss the shrimp with the olive oil until it's well coated.
- Coat the shrimp with the spice mixture.
- Place the shrimp on the skewer rack and place it in your air fryer and allow them to cook for 5 minutes.
- Serve the cooked shrimp with the side of your choice.

Air Fryer Accessories Recipe Cookbook

# Crispy Coconut Shrimp with Spicy Citrus Sauce

Prep Time: 10 Minutes / Cook Time: 20 Minutes / Servings: 2
Use the Skewer Rack

## INGREDIENTS FOR MAKING THIS RECIPE:

*8 large shrimp, shelled and deveined*
*8 ounces coconut milk*
*1/2 cup shredded, sweetened coconut*
*1/2 cup panko bread*
*1/2 teaspoon cayenne pepper*
*1/4 teaspoon kosher salt*
*1/4 teaspoon fresh ground pepper*

*Citrus Sauce:*
*1/2 cup orange marmalade*
*1 tablespoon honey*
*1 teaspoon mustard*
*1/4 teaspoon hot sauce*

*Cooking spray*

## DIRECTIONS FOR PREPARING THIS RECIPE:

- Spray the basket of your air fryer with cooking spray.
- Preheat your air fryer to 350F.
- Place the coconut milk in a bowl along with salt and pepper to taste. Use a whisk to mix the ingredients.
- Place the shredded coconut in a different bowl with the panko, cayenne, and salt and pepper. Use a whisk to mix the ingredients together.
- Coat the shrimp with the coconut milk and coat it with the panko mixture.
- Place the shrimp on the skewer rack and place it in your air fryer and cook for 20 minutes or a few minutes longer if not completely cooked.
- Place the sauce ingredient in a bowl and use a whisk to combine them, while the shrimp is cooking.
- Serve the cooked shrimp with a side of the spicy citrus sauce.

By Alicia Patterson

# Sweet Citrus Salmon

Prep Time: 10 Minutes / Cook Time: 10 Minutes / Servings: 2

## INGREDIENTS FOR MAKING THIS RECIPE:

*8 oz. salmon filets cut into 4 oz. portions*
*1/2 tsp Lemon Pepper*
*1 tsp Turbinado sugar or dark brown sugar*
*2 dashes Extra Virgin Olive Oil*

*Sauce*
*1/4 cup plain low fat yogurt Greek style is preferred*
*1/2 tsp dill weed*
*1/4 tsp garlic powder*
*1/2 tsp lemon zest*

*2 sprig Fresh dill to garnish top of salmon*
*2 wedges lemon to garnish and squeeze onto salmon*

## DIRECTIONS FOR PREPARING THIS RECIPE:

- Preheat your air fryer to 400F for at least 4 minutes.
- Season the salmon with the lemon pepper and sugar.
- Give the salmon a light coating of olive oil.
- Place the salmon in your air fryer and allow it cook for 10 minutes.
- While the salmon is cooking, mix together the sauce ingredients in a medium sized bowl.
- Top the cooked salmon with a dollop of the sauce and then a sprig of fresh dill.
- Serve with a lemon wedge for squeezing and the side of your choice.

Air Fryer Accessories Recipe Cookbook

# Soy Lemon Sugar Salmon

Prep Time: 2 Hours 10 Minutes / Cook Time: 8 Minutes / Servings: 2

## INGREDIENTS FOR MAKING THIS RECIPE:

*2, 8-ounce Salmon fillets*
*garlic powder, black pepper and salt to taste*

*Marinade:*
*1/3 cup light soy sauce*
*1/3 cup brown sugar*
*1/3 cup water*
*fresh squeezed lemon juice from 1 large lemon*

*2 tablespoons olive oil*
*scallion slices and cherry tomato for garnish*

## DIRECTIONS FOR PREPARING THIS RECIPE:

- Rinse the salmon and use paper towels to pat it dry. Use salt, pepper, and garlic powder to season the salmon to your taste.
- Mix the marinade ingredients in a bowl. Add in the salmon, cover the bowl, and allow it to marinate refrigerator for a minimum of 2 hours.
- Preheat your air fryer to 355F.
- Put the marinated salmon in your air fryer and cook it for 8 minutes.
- Serve the cooked salmon with a garnish of sliced scallion and cherry tomato.

By Alicia Patterson

# Crab Cake Sliders

Prep Time: 5 Minutes / Cook Time: 10 Minutes / Servings: 4

## INGREDIENTS FOR MAKING THIS RECIPE:

*8 ounces of jumbo lump crab meat*
*1/3 cup whole wheat bread crumbs*
*¼ cup red peppers diced*
*¼ cup green peppers diced*
*1 medium egg*
*¼ cup reduced fat mayo*
*½ lemon juice of*
*1 teaspoon flour*
*1 tablespoon Old Bay Seasoning*
*cooking oil*
*slider buns*

## DIRECTIONS FOR PREPARING THIS RECIPE:

- Preheat your air fryer to 375F.
- Place all the ingredients except for the cooking oil, buns and flour in a bowl. Mix them together until well combined.
- Make the mixture into 8 slider sized patties. Sprinkle them with a little flour.
- Put the patties in your air fryer and give them a light spritz with the cooking oil. Allow the patties to cook for 10 minutes.
- Place the patties in the slider buns to serve.

Air Fryer Accessories Recipe Cookbook

# Crab Fried Rice

Prep Time: 10 Minutes / Cook Time: 20 Minutes / Servings: 6

## INGREDIENTS FOR MAKING THIS RECIPE:

3 cups white rice cold, cooked
1 cup frozen peas and carrots
6 tbsps. soy sauce
1 tbsp. vegetable oil
1/2 cup onion diced
1 cup lump crab meat
Cooking spray

## DIRECTIONS FOR PREPARING THIS RECIPE:

* Preheat your air fryer to 360F.
* Put the rice in a bowl and mix in the oil and soy sauce. Make sure all ingredients are well mixed.
* Mix in the onions, crab, peas and carrots. Make sure all ingredients are well mixed again.
* Put the mixture in a non-stick pan that's small enough to fit in your air fryer if you have one. If not spray cooking in a pan smaller enough to fit in your air fryer before adding in the mixture.
* Put the pan into your air fryer and allow it cook for 20 minutes.
* Once it's cooked, place the rice in a bowl or on a plate to serve.

By Alicia Patterson

# Lobster Tails with Lemon Garlic Butter

Prep Time: 10 Minutes / Cook Time: 6 Minutes / Servings: 2

## INGREDIENTS FOR MAKING THIS RECIPE:

*4 lobster tails*

*Lemon Garlic Butter:*
*2 tablespoons butter*
*1 tbsp. Lemon Juice*
*Salt, to taste*
*Pepper, to taste*
*2 tsps. Minced garlic*

## DIRECTIONS FOR PREPARING THIS RECIPE:

- Preheat your air fryer to 380F.
- Heat a small sauce pan on medium heat and add in the butter. Let the butter melt and add in the garlic. Let the garlic cook for about 30 seconds until it becomes fragrant. Take the butter of the heat and mix in the lemon juice and salt and pepper to taste.
- Use kitchen scissors to carefully cut open the lobster tails. Then carefully break and pull back the shell to expose the meat.
- Brush the lobster tails with the lemon garlic butter.
- Put the lobster in your air fryer and cook them for 4 minutes. After the 4 minutes, brush the lobster with any leftover lemon garlic butter and cook for 2 additional minutes.

Air Fryer Accessories Recipe Cookbook

# Keto Friendly Shrimp Scampi

Prep Time: 2 Hours 10 Minutes / Cook Time: 8 Minutes / Servings: 2

## INGREDIENTS FOR MAKING THIS RECIPE:

*4 tablespoons butter*
*1 tablespoon lemon juice*
*1 tablespoon minced garlic*
*2 teaspoons red pepper flakes*
*1 tablespoon chopped chives or 1 teaspoon dried chives*
*1 tablespoon minced basil leaves plus more for sprinkling or 1 teaspoon dried basil*
*2 tablespoons chicken stock or white wine*
*1 pound shrimp, peeled and deveined*

## DIRECTIONS FOR PREPARING THIS RECIPE:

- Set your air fryer to 330F. Put 6x3 metal pan in the basket before it heats up.
- Once the air fryer reaches 330F, add the red pepper, butter, and garlic to the metal pan.
- Allow the mixture to cook for 2 minutes, making sure to stir the mixture once during the cooking process.
- Add in the chives, then basil, then stock or wine, and finally the shrimp. Cook the mixture for 5 minutes, making sure to stir the mixture once during the cooking process.
- Allow the cooked mixture to rest for 1 minute before stirring again.
- Top with more basil for garnish and serve.

By Alicia Patterson

# Bacon Wrapped Scallops

Prep Time: 20 Minutes / Cook Time: 6 Minutes / Servings: 4

## INGREDIENTS FOR MAKING THIS RECIPE:

*20 Raw Sea Scallops,*
*5 slices Center-Cut Bacon*
*1 tsp lemon pepper seasoning*
*1 tsp Paprika*
*Cooking Spray*
*20 toothpicks*

## DIRECTIONS FOR PREPARING THIS RECIPE:

- Preheat your air fryer to 400F.
- Spray the basket with cooking spray.
- Rinse the scallops and lay them between 2 paper towels to dry and absorb any excess moisture.
- Cut every slice of bacon into 4 equal sized pieces.
- Wrap 1 the smaller pieces of bacon around 1 of the scallops and use a toothpick to hold it in place. Repeat with the remaining scallops and bacon.
- Season both sides of the exposed scallop with paprika and lemon pepper.
- Place the scallops in your air fryer give them a light mist of cooking spray and cook for 5-6 minutes.
- Remove the toothpicks from the cooked scallops and serve.

Air Fryer Accessories Recipe Cookbook

# Before You Go Further!

## We Need Your Help... ☺

## PLEASE LEAVE US AN AMAZON REVIEW!

If you were pleased with our book then leave us a review on Amazon where you purchased this book! **Here's the web link to leave a review.**
**Simply type the link to your web browser,** scroll to the bottom & review!

### >>> Amazon.com/dp/B07FK96P57 <<<

In the world of an author who writes books independently, your reviews are not only touching but important so that we know you like the material we have prepared for "you" our audience! So, leave us a review...we would love to see that you enjoyed our book!

If for any reason that you were less than happy with your experience then send me an email at **Info@RecipeNerds.com** and let me know how we can better your experience. We always come out with a few volumes of our books and will possibly be able to address some of your concerns. Do keep in mind that we strive to do our best to give you the highest quality of what "we the independent authors" pour our heart and tears into.

Hello all...I am very excited that you have purchased one of my publications. Please feel free to give us an amazon review where you purchased the book! If you already have, then I thank you for your many great reviews and comments! With a warm heart! ~Alicia Patterson "Personal & Professional Chef"

By Alicia Patterson

# Sides

Air Fryer Accessories Recipe Cookbook

# Asparagus with Basil & Olive Oil

Prep Time: 5 Minutes / Cook Time: 10 Minutes / Servings: 2
Use the Steel Metal Holder

## INGREDIENTS FOR MAKING THIS RECIPE:

½ bunch asparagus
1 tsp. basil
Salt to taste
Avocado or olive oil in a spray bottle

## DIRECTIONS FOR PREPARING THIS RECIPE:

- Trim the ends of your asparagus.
- Put half the asparagus in the basket of your air fryer, put in the holder, and the remaining asparagus, and lightly spray it with the oil then sprinkle the basil on. Season with salt to taste.
- Put the basket back in your air fryer and cook for 10 minutes at 400F.

By Alicia Patterson

# Asparagus with Lemon Pepper

Prep Time: 5 Minutes / Cook Time: 10 Minutes / Servings: 2

Use the Steel Metal Holder

## INGREDIENTS FOR MAKING THIS RECIPE:

½ bunch asparagus
Lemon pepper
Salt to taste
Avocado or olive oil in a spray bottle

## DIRECTIONS FOR PREPARING THIS RECIPE:

- Trim the ends of your asparagus.
- Put half the asparagus in the basket of your air fryer, put in the metal holder, add the remaining asparagus, and lightly spray it with the oil. Season with lemon pepper and salt to taste.
- Put the basket back in your air fryer and cook for 10 minutes at 400F.

Air Fryer Accessories Recipe Cookbook

# Asparagus with Carrots

Prep Time: 5 Minutes / Cook Time: 10 Minutes / Servings: 2

## INGREDIENTS FOR MAKING THIS RECIPE:

*½ bunch asparagus*
*3 full carrots*
*Salt to taste*
*Avocado or olive oil in a spray bottle*

## DIRECTIONS FOR PREPARING THIS RECIPE:

* Trim the ends of your asparagus and cut the carrots into strips as thin as the asparagus.
* Put half the asparagus and carrots in the basket of your air fryer, put in the holder, add the remaining asparagus and carrots, and lightly spray it with the oil. Season with salt to taste.
* Put the basket back in your air fryer and cook for 10 minutes at 400F.
* Serve immediately.

By Alicia Patterson

# Honey Carrots

Prep Time: 5 Minutes / Cook Time: 10 Minutes / Servings: 2
Use the Steel Metal Holder

## INGREDIENTS FOR MAKING THIS RECIPE:

3 cups of baby carrots or regular carrots cut into large pieces
1 tbsp. Olive oil
1 tbsp. Honey
Salt and pepper to taste

## DIRECTIONS FOR PREPARING THIS RECIPE:

- Preheat your air fryer to 200F.
- Mix the carrots, honey and olive oil together in a bowl until carrots are completely covered.
- Season the carrots with salt and pepper to taste.
- Put half the carrots in your air fryer, then the holder, add in the remaining carrots, and allow them to cook for 12 minutes.
- Serve immediately.

Air Fryer Accessories Recipe Cookbook

# Asian Cauliflower Carrots

Prep Time: 5 Minutes / Cook Time: 10 Minutes / Servings: 2
Use the Steel Metal Holder

## INGREDIENTS FOR MAKING THIS RECIPE:

*3 cups of baby carrots or regular carrots cut into large pieces*
*½ cauliflower*
*1 tbsp. Olive oil*
*1 tbsp. Soy Sauce*
*Pepper to taste*

## DIRECTIONS FOR PREPARING THIS RECIPE:

- Preheat your air fryer to 200F.
- Mix the carrots, cauliflower, honey, soy sauce and olive oil together in a bowl until vegetables are completely covered.
- Put half the vegetables in your air fryer, add in the holder, put in the remaining vegetables, and allow them to cook for 12 minutes.
- Season the vegetables with pepper to taste.
- Serve immediately.

By Alicia Patterson

# Fried Pickles

Prep Time: 10 Minutes / Cook Time: 10 Minutes / Servings: 2

## INGREDIENTS FOR MAKING THIS RECIPE:

*2 c. dill pickle slices*
*1 egg, whisked with 1 tbsp. water*
*3/4 c. breadcrumbs*
*1/4 c. freshly grated parmesan*
*1 tsp. dried oregano*
*Ranch, for dipping*
*Cooking spray*

## DIRECTIONS FOR PREPARING THIS RECIPE:

- Spray the basket of your air fryer with cooking spray.
- Preheat your air fryer to 360F.
- Pat the pickles dry using a paper towel.
- Mix together the parmesan, oregano and breadcrumbs in bowl until well combined.
- Coat the pickles with the egg mixture and then the parmesan breadcrumb mixture.
- Place the pickles in your air fryer and cook for 10 minutes flipping halfway through.
- Serve immediately with a side of ranch.

Air Fryer Accessories Recipe Cookbook

# Garlic Fried Pickles

Prep Time: 10 Minutes / Cook Time: 10 Minutes / Servings: 2

## INGREDIENTS FOR MAKING THIS RECIPE:

*2 c. dill pickle slices*
*1 egg, whisked with 1 tbsp. water*
*3/4 c. breadcrumbs*
*1/4 c. freshly grated parmesan*
*1 tsp. dried oregano*
*1 tsp. garlic powder*
*Ranch or honey mustard, for dipping*
*Cooking spray*

## DIRECTIONS FOR PREPARING THIS RECIPE:

- Spray the basket of your air fryer with cooking spray.
- Preheat your air fryer to 360F.
- Pat the pickles dry using a paper towel.
- Mix together the parmesan, oregano, breadcrumbs, and garlic powder in bowl until well combined.
- Coat the pickles with the egg mixture and then the parmesan breadcrumb mixture.
- Place the pickles in your air fryer and cook for 10 minutes flipping halfway through.
- Serve immediately with a side of ranch.

By Alicia Patterson

# Spicy Fried Pickles

Prep Time: 10 Minutes / Cook Time: 10 Minutes / Servings: 2

## INGREDIENTS FOR MAKING THIS RECIPE:

*2 c. dill pickle slices*
*1 egg, whisked with 1 tbsp. water*
*3/4 c. breadcrumbs*
*1/4 c. freshly grated parmesan*
*1 tsp. dried oregano*
*1 tsp. garlic powder*
*¼ teaspoon cayenne pepper*
*Ranch, for dipping*
*Cooking spray*

## DIRECTIONS FOR PREPARING THIS RECIPE:

* Spray the basket of your air fryer with cooking spray.
* Preheat your air fryer to 360F.
* Pat the pickles dry using a paper towel.
* Mix together the parmesan, oregano, breadcrumbs, cayenne pepper and garlic powder in bowl until well combined.
* Coat the pickles with the egg mixture and then the parmesan breadcrumb mixture.
* Place the pickles in your air fryer and cook for 10 minutes flipping halfway through.
* Serve immediately with a side of ranch.

Air Fryer Accessories Recipe Cookbook

# Golden Crisp French Fries

Prep Time: 10 Minutes / Cook Time: 10 Minutes / Servings: 4
Use the Steel Metal Holder

## INGREDIENTS FOR MAKING THIS RECIPE:

*2 medium peeled potatoes, about 12 ounces total weight*
*2 teaspoons olive oil*
*1/2 tsp kosher salt*
*fresh black pepper, to taste*

## DIRECTIONS FOR PREPARING THIS RECIPE:

- Preheat your air fryer to 400F for at least 8 minutes.
- Spray the basket of your air fryer and the steel metal holder with a little oil.
- Cut the potatoes into ¼ inch thick sticks.
- Place the 2 teaspoons of oil and spices in a bowl and mix them together. Add in the potatoes and toss until well coated.
- Place half the potatoes in your air fryer and then the steel metal holder. Place the remaining fries on the holder. Cook for 8 – 10 minutes flipping the fries over halfway through.

By Alicia Patterson

# Golden Scallion Garlic Fries

Prep Time: 10 Minutes / Cook Time: 10 Minutes / Servings: 4
Use the Steel Metal Holder

## INGREDIENTS FOR MAKING THIS RECIPE:

*2 medium peeled potatoes, about 12 ounces total weight*
*2 teaspoons olive oil*
*1 tablespoons finely chopped scallions*
*2 tablespoons minced garlic*
*1/2 tsp kosher salt*
*fresh black pepper, to taste*

## DIRECTIONS FOR PREPARING THIS RECIPE:

- Preheat your air fryer to 400F for at least 8 minutes.
- Spray the basket of your air fryer and the metal holder with a little oil.
- Cut the potatoes into ¼ inch thick sticks.
- Place the 2 teaspoons of oil and spices in a bowl and mix them together. Add in the potatoes and toss until well coated.
- Place half the potatoes in your air fryer and then the steel metal holder. Place the remaining fries on the holder. Cook for 8 – 10 minutes flipping the fries over halfway through.

Air Fryer Accessories Recipe Cookbook

# Parmesan Fries

Prep Time: 10 Minutes / Cook Time: 10 Minutes / Servings: 4
Use the Steel Metal Holder

## INGREDIENTS FOR MAKING THIS RECIPE:

2 medium peeled potatoes, about 12 ounces total weight
2 teaspoons olive oil
1 tablespoons finely chopped scallions
1 cup Parmesan cheese
1/2 tsp kosher salt
fresh black pepper, to taste

## DIRECTIONS FOR PREPARING THIS RECIPE:

- Preheat your air fryer to 400F for at least 8 minutes.
- Spray the basket of your air fryer and the metal holder with a little oil.
- Cut the potatoes into ¼ inch thick sticks.
- Place the 2 teaspoons of oil and spices in a bowl and mix them together. Add in the potatoes and toss until well coated.
- Place half the potatoes in your air fryer and then the steel metal holder. Place the remaining fries on the holder. Cook for 8 – 10 minutes flipping the fries over halfway through.
- When done, take 1 light spray of oil over the hot fries then sprinkle the parmesan cheese over the top of the fries in abundance!

By Alicia Patterson

# Garlic Parmesan Fries

Prep Time: 10 Minutes / Cook Time: 10 Minutes / Servings: 4

Use the Steel Metal Holder

## INGREDIENTS FOR MAKING THIS RECIPE:

2 medium peeled potatoes, about 12 ounces total weight
2 teaspoons olive oil
1 tablespoons finely chopped scallions
1 cup Parmesan cheese
2 tablespoons minced garlic
1/2 tsp kosher salt
fresh black pepper, to taste

## DIRECTIONS FOR PREPARING THIS RECIPE:

- Preheat your air fryer to 400F for at least 8 minutes.
- Spray the basket of your air fryer and metal holder with a little oil.
- Cut the potatoes into ¼ inch thick sticks.
- Place the 2 teaspoons of oil and spices in a bowl and mix them together. Add in the potatoes and toss until well coated.
- Place half the potatoes in your air fryer and then the steel metal holder. Place the remaining fries on the holder. Cook for 8 – 10 minutes flipping the fries over halfway through.
- When done, take 1 light spray of oil over the hot fries then sprinkle the parmesan cheese over the top of the fries in abundance!

Air Fryer Accessories Recipe Cookbook

# Garlic Parmesan Jalapeño Fries

Prep Time: 10 Minutes / Cook Time: 10 Minutes / Servings: 4
Use the Steel Metal Holder

## INGREDIENTS FOR MAKING THIS RECIPE:

2 medium peeled potatoes, about 12 ounces total weight
2 teaspoons olive oil
2 diced jalapeno peppers
1 tablespoons finely chopped scallions
1 cup Parmesan cheese
2 tablespoons minced garlic
1/2 tsp kosher salt
fresh black pepper, to taste

## DIRECTIONS FOR PREPARING THIS RECIPE:

- Preheat your air fryer to 400F for at least 8 minutes.
- Spray the basket of your air fryer and metal holder with a little oil.
- Cut the potatoes into ¼ inch thick sticks.
- Place the 2 teaspoons of oil and spices in a bowl and mix them together. Add in the potatoes and toss until well coated.
- Place half the potatoes in your air fryer and then the steel metal holder. Place the remaining fries on the holder. Cook for 8 – 10 minutes flipping the fries over halfway through.
- When done, dump the fries into a large bowl. Take 1 light spray of oil over the hot crisp fries. Add the garlic, jalapeños and parmesan cheese over the top of the fries. Toss well and serve hot!

By Alicia Patterson

# Sweet Potato Fries

Prep Time: 10 Minutes / Cook Time: 10 Minutes / Servings: 4
Use the Steel Metal Holder

## INGREDIENTS FOR MAKING THIS RECIPE:

2 medium peeled sweet potatoes, about 12 ounces total weight
2 teaspoons olive oil
1/2 tsp kosher salt
1/4 teaspoon sweet paprika
fresh black pepper, to taste

## DIRECTIONS FOR PREPARING THIS RECIPE:

- Preheat your air fryer to 400F for at least 8 minutes.
- Spray the basket of your air fryer and metal holder with a little oil.
- Cut the sweet potatoes into ¼ inch thick sticks.
- Place the 2 teaspoons of oil and spices in a bowl and mix them together. Add in the sweet potatoes and toss until well coated.
- Place half the potatoes in your air fryer and then the steel metal holder. Place the remaining fries on the holder. Cook for 8 minutes flipping the fries over halfway through.

Air Fryer Accessories Recipe Cookbook

# Spicy Sweet Potato Fries

Prep Time: 10 Minutes / Cook Time: 10 Minutes / Servings: 4
Use the Steel Metal Holder

## INGREDIENTS FOR MAKING THIS RECIPE:

*2 medium peeled sweet potatoes, about 12 ounces total weight*
*2 teaspoons olive oil*
*1/2 tsp kosher salt*
*1/2 teaspoon garlic powder*
*1/4 teaspoon sweet paprika*
*¼ teaspoon cayenne pepper*
*fresh black pepper, to taste*

## DIRECTIONS FOR PREPARING THIS RECIPE:

- Preheat your air fryer to 400F for at least 8 minutes.
- Spray the basket of your air fryer and metal holder with a little oil.
- Cut the sweet potatoes into ¼ inch thick sticks.
- Place the 2 teaspoons of oil and spices in a bowl and mix them together. Add in the sweet potatoes and toss until well coated.
- Place half the potatoes in your air fryer and then the steel metal holder. Place the remaining fries on the holder. Cook for 8 minutes flipping the fries over halfway through.

88

By Alicia Patterson

# Truffle Parmesan Fries

Prep Time: 10 Minutes / Cook Time: 10 Minutes / Servings: 2
Use the Steel Metal Holder

## INGREDIENTS FOR MAKING THIS RECIPE:

3 medium russet potatoes
2 tbsps. parmesan cheese
2 tbsps. finely chopped fresh parsley
1 tbsp. olive oil
Truffle salt
Cooking spray

## DIRECTIONS FOR PREPARING THIS RECIPE:

- Preheat your air fryer to 360F for at least 3 minutes.
- Spray the basket of your air fryer and metal holder with cooking spray.
- Cut the potatoes into ¼ inch thick sticks.
- Use a paper towel to pat the potatoes dry.
- Place the f oil and spices in a bowl and mix them together. Add in the potatoes and toss until well coated.
- Place the potatoes in your air fryer and cook for 20 minutes. Flip the fries at the 10-minute mark and again at the 15 minute mark.
- Serve immediately.

Air Fryer Accessories Recipe Cookbook

# Garlic Parmesan Roasted Potatoes

Prep Time: 10 Minutes / Cook Time: 20 Minutes / Servings: 6

## INGREDIENTS FOR MAKING THIS RECIPE:

½ teaspoon dried basil
5 cloves garlic, minced
½ teaspoon dried oregano,
2 tablespoons parsley leaves
3 pounds red potatoes
1 teaspoon dried thyme
Kosher salt and freshly ground black pepper, to taste
2 tablespoons olive oil
2 tablespoons butter, unsalted and melted
⅓ cup grated Parmesan cheese
1 sheet of baking paper

## DIRECTIONS FOR PREPARING THIS RECIPE:

- Put a sheet of baking paper in the basket of your air fryer.
- Preheat your air fryer to 400F.
- Wash the potatoes and pat them dry with paper towels.
- Slice the potatoes into quarters.
- Put all the ingredients into a bowl and mix well.
- Add in the potatoes and toss until well coated.
- Put the potatoes in your air fryer and allow them to cook for 18-20 minutes. Flip the potatoes after 10 minutes.
- Serve immediately.

By Alicia Patterson

# Turmeric Tofu and Cauliflower Rice

Prep Time: 10 Minutes / Cook Time: 20 Minutes / Servings: 6

## INGREDIENTS FOR MAKING THIS RECIPE:

*Tofu:*
1/2 block firm or extra firm tofu
2 tablespoons reduced sodium soy sauce
1/2 cup diced onion
1 cup diced carrot about 1 1/2 to 2 carrots
1 teaspoon turmeric

*Cauliflower Rice:*
3 cups riced cauliflower
 2 tablespoons reduced sodium soy sauce
1 1/2 teaspoons toasted sesame oil optional,
1 tablespoon rice vinegar
1 tablespoon minced ginger
1/2 cup finely chopped broccoli
2 cloves garlic minced
1/2 cup frozen peas

## DIRECTIONS FOR PREPARING THIS RECIPE:

- Preheat your air fryer to 370F.
- Crumble the tofu into small pieces into a bug bowl. Add in the remaining tofu ingredients and mix well.
- Place the mixture in your air fryer and cook for 10 minutes. Shake the mixture halfway through.
- While the tofu mixture is cooking, place the cauliflower rice ingredients in the bowl you mixed the tofu in. Mix the ingredients together until they're well combined.
- Place the cooked tofu ingredients in a serving bowl and set aside.
- Place the cauliflower rice ingredients in your air fryer and cook for 10 minutes. Shake the mixture halfway through. If the rice isn't cooked through after 10 minutes cook for an additional 2-5 minutes.
- Place the cooked rice in the bowl with the tofu and toss until well combined.

Air Fryer Accessories Recipe Cookbook

# Fried Ravioli with Marinara Sauce

Prep Time: 10 Minutes / Cook Time: 5 Minutes / Servings: 6

## INGREDIENTS FOR MAKING THIS RECIPE:

1, 14-ounce jar marinara sauce
1, 9-ounce box cheese ravioli or meat ravioli, store-bought
1 teaspoon olive oil
2 cups Italian-style bread crumbs
1 cup buttermilk
¼ cup Parmesan cheese
1 sheet of baking paper

## DIRECTIONS FOR PREPARING THIS RECIPE:

* Put a sheet of baking paper in the basket of your air fryer.
* Preheat your air fryer to 200F.
* Put the breadcrumbs and olive oil in a bowl and mix them together. Place the buttermilk in a bowl.
* Dip the ravioli in the buttermilk and then coat them with the breadcrumb mixture.
* Place the ravioli in your air fryer and cook for 5 minutes.
* While the ravioli is cooking, heat up some marinara sauce in the stove or in the microwave.
* Serve the ravioli with a side of the marinara.

By Alicia Patterson

# Avocado Fries with Lime Dip

Prep Time: 10 Minutes / Cook Time: 8 Minutes / Servings: 2

## INGREDIENTS FOR MAKING THIS RECIPE:

*Avocado Fries:*
*8 ounces (2 small) avocados, peeled, pitted and cut into 16 wedges*
*1 large egg, lightly beaten*
*3/4 cup panko breadcrumbs*
*1 1/4 teaspoons lime chili seasoning salt, like Tajin Classic*

*Lime Dipping Sauce:*
*1/4 cup Greek Yogurt*
*3 tablespoons light mayonnaise*
*2 teaspoons fresh lime juice*
*1/2 teaspoon lime chili seasoning salt, such as Tajin Classic*
*1/8 teaspoon kosher salt*

Cooking Spray

## DIRECTIONS FOR PREPARING THIS RECIPE:

- Spray the basket of your air fryer with cooking spray.
- Preheat your air fryer to 390F.
- Mix the panko and lime chili seasoning in a bowl. Place egg in a small bowl.
- Coat the avocado with the egg and then with the panko mixture.
- Place the avocado fries in your air fryer and cook for 7-8 minutes. Flip the fries halfway through the cooking process.
- While the avocado fries are cooking, Place all the lime dip ingredients in a bowl. Mix them together until well combined.
- Serve the fries immediately with the lime dipping sauce.

Air Fryer Accessories Recipe Cookbook

# Stuffed Mushrooms

Prep Time: 10 Minutes / Cook Time: 8 Minutes / Servings: 2

## INGREDIENTS FOR MAKING THIS RECIPE:

*10 ounces fresh white mushrooms*
*1 cup flour*
*½ cup cornstarch*
*¾ teaspoon baking powder*
*1 teaspoon seasoning salt*
*1 cup water*
*2 cups panko breadcrumbs*

Cooking Spray

## DIRECTIONS FOR PREPARING THIS RECIPE:

- Spray the basket of your air fryer with cooking spray.
- Preheat your air fryer to 360F.
- Wipe off the mushrooms to make sure they're clean.
- In a bowl, combine the cornstarch, salt, baking powder, and flour. Make sure they're well mixed. Pour in the water and stir to combine everything. Place the panko in a separate bowl.
- Coat the mushrooms with the cornstarch mixture and then coat it with the panko.
- Place the mushrooms in your air fryer and cook them for 7 minutes. Make sure you shake the basket halfway through cooking.
- Serve immediately.

By Alicia Patterson

# Honey Glazed Button Mushrooms

Prep Time: 10 Minutes / Cook Time: 8 Minutes / Servings: 2

Use the Steel Metal Holder

## INGREDIENTS FOR MAKING THIS RECIPE:

*10-12 ounces fresh white mushrooms*
*1 teaspoon seasoning salt*
*1 tablespoon Dijon mustard*
*1 teaspoon honey*
*pepper to taste*
Cooking spray oil

## DIRECTIONS FOR PREPARING THIS RECIPE:

* Spray the basket of your air fryer with cooking spray.
* Preheat your air fryer to 360F.
* Wipe off the mushrooms to make sure they're clean.
* Spray mushrooms with light oil.
* In a bowl, add mushrooms, pepper, salt and toss.
* Place the mushrooms in your air fryer and cook them for 5 minutes. Make sure you shake the basket halfway through cooking.
* Coat or brush the mushrooms with the Dijon/honey mixture.
* Place back into the air fryer for another 3 minutes.
* Serve immediately.

Air Fryer Accessories Recipe Cookbook

# Zucchini Fries

Prep Time: 10 Minutes / Cook Time: 8 Minutes / Servings: 3

## INGREDIENTS FOR MAKING THIS RECIPE:

**Roasted Garlic Aïoli:**
1 teaspoon roasted garlic
2 tablespoons olive oil
½ cup mayonnaise
juice of ½ lemon
salt and pepper

**Zucchini Fries:**
½ cup flour
2 eggs, beaten
1 cup seasoned breadcrumbs
salt and pepper
1 large zucchini, cut into ½-inch sticks
olive oil in a spray bottle, can or mister

## DIRECTIONS FOR PREPARING THIS RECIPE:

- Put the flour in one bowl, the egg in another bowl, and the breadcrumbs and salt and pepper to taste in a 3rd bowl.
- Dip the zucchini in the flour, then egg, and finally the seasoned bread crumbs.
- Let the zucchini rest for about 10 minutes.
- While the zucchini is resting, preheat your air fryer to 400F.
- Spray the fries lightly with the olive oil spray and put them in your air fryer. Cook the fries for 12 minutes, flipping them halfway through.
- While the zucchini is cooking, whisk together all the aioli ingredients together except for the salt and pepper in a bowl. When they're well mixed, add salt and pepper to taste.
- Serve the zucchini fries with the aioli.

By Alicia Patterson

# Shishito Peppers with Asiago Cheese

Prep Time: 10 Minutes / Cook Time: 10 Minutes / Servings: 4

## INGREDIENTS FOR MAKING THIS RECIPE:

*6 ounces shishito peppers*
*salt and pepper to taste*
*1/2 tablespoon avocado oil*
*1/3 cups Asiago cheese, grated fine*
*limes*

## DIRECTIONS FOR PREPARING THIS RECIPE:

- Clean the peppers by rinsing them with some water and using a paper towel to pat them dry.
- Preheat your air fryer to 350F.
- Put the oil in a bowl along with the peppers and toss until well coated. Season with salt and pepper to taste.
- Place in the peppers in your air fryer and cook them for 10 minutes. Keep an eye on them during the last couple mints so that they blister but don't burn
- Squeeze lime juice on the cooked peppers and top with cheese to serve.

Air Fryer Accessories Recipe Cookbook

# Salt & Vinegar Chips

Prep Time: 25 Minutes / Cook Time: 12 Minutes Servings: 3

## INGREDIENTS FOR MAKING THIS RECIPE:

*5 baby yellow potatoes, thinly sliced*
*1 cup apple cider vinegar*
*½ tablespoon extra-virgin olive oil*
*½ teaspoon sea salt*

## DIRECTIONS FOR PREPARING THIS RECIPE:

* Place the apple cider vinegar and potatoes in the bowl. Mix them together and let them marinate together for 15 minutes.
* Preheat your air fryer to 360F.
* In a separate bowl mix together the remaining ingredients. Take the potatoes out of the vinegar and place them in this bowl. Toss together until the potatoes are well coated.
* Place the potatoes in your air fryer and cook for 12 minutes. Check the potatoes every 3 minutes to ensure they're cooking properly.
* Allow them to cool for a few minutes and serve.

By Alicia Patterson

# Beet Chips

Prep Time: 20 Minutes / Cook Time: 1 Hour 5 Minutes / Servings: 4
Use the Steel Metal Holder

## INGREDIENTS FOR MAKING THIS RECIPE:

*3 medium-size red beets about 1 1/2 pounds, peeled and cut into 1/8-inch thick slices
(about 3 cups slices)
2 teaspoons canola oil
3/4 teaspoon kosher salt
1/4 teaspoon black pepper*

## DIRECTIONS FOR PREPARING THIS RECIPE:

- Slice the beets into 1/8 inch pieces using a knife or a mandoline if you have one.
- Preheat your air fryer to 320F.
- Place the beets in a bowl with the remaining ingredients and toss until the beats are well coated,
- Place the beats in your air fryer in 2 separate batches and cook each batch for 25-30 minutes. Make sure to shake the basket about every 5 minutes.
- Allow the chips to cool for a few minutes before serving.

Air Fryer Accessories Recipe Cookbook

# Potato Chips

Prep Time: 20 Minutes / Cook Time: 1 Hour 5 Minutes / Servings: 4
Use the Steel Metal Holder

## INGREDIENTS FOR MAKING THIS RECIPE:

3 medium-size Potatoes about 1 1/2 pounds, peeled and cut into 1/8-inch thick slices
(about 3 cups slices)
2 teaspoons coconut oil (or avocado oil)
3/4 teaspoon kosher salt
1/4 teaspoon black pepper

## DIRECTIONS FOR PREPARING THIS RECIPE:

- Slice the beets into 1/8 inch pieces using a knife or a mandoline if you have one.
- Preheat your air fryer to 320F.
- Place the potatoes in a bowl with the remaining ingredients and toss until the potatoes are well coated,
- Place half the potatoes in your air fryer and place the metal holder in your air fryer. Place the remaining potatoes on the holder and cook for 25-30 minutes. Make sure to shake the basket about every 5 minutes.
- Allow the chips to cool for a few minutes before serving.

By Alicia Patterson

# Parmesan Potato Chips

Prep Time: 20 Minutes / Cook Time: 1 Hour 5 Minutes / Servings: 4

## INGREDIENTS FOR MAKING THIS RECIPE:

*3 medium-size Potatoes about 1 1/2 pounds, peeled and cut into 1/8-inch thick slices (about 3 cups slices)*
*2 teaspoons coconut oil (or avocado oil)*
*2 tablespoons grated parmesan cheese*
*3/4 teaspoon kosher salt*
*1/4 teaspoon black pepper*

## DIRECTIONS FOR PREPARING THIS RECIPE:

- Slice the beets into 1/8 inch pieces using a knife or a mandoline if you have one.
- Preheat your air fryer to 320F.
- Place the potatoes in a bowl with the remaining ingredients and toss until the potatoes are well coated,
- Place half the potatoes in your air fryer and place the metal holder in your air fryer. Place the remaining potatoes on the holder and cook for 25-30 minutes. Make sure to shake the basket about every 5 minutes.
- Toss the chips into a large bowl and sprinkle on the parmesan cheese.
- Allow the chips to cool for a few minutes before serving.

Air Fryer Accessories Recipe Cookbook

# Garlic Parmesan Potato Chips

Prep Time: 20 Minutes / Cook Time: 1 Hour 5 Minutes /Servings: 4

## INGREDIENTS FOR MAKING THIS RECIPE:

*3 medium-size Potatoes about 1 1/2 pounds, peeled and cut into 1/8-inch thick slices
(about 3 cups slices)*
*1 tablespoon minced garlic*
*2 teaspoons coconut oil (or avocado oil)*
*2 tablespoons grated parmesan cheese*
*3/4 teaspoon kosher salt*
*1/4 teaspoon black pepper*

## DIRECTIONS FOR PREPARING THIS RECIPE:

- Slice the beets into 1/8 inch pieces using a knife or a mandoline if you have one.
- Preheat your air fryer to 320F.
- Place the potatoes in a bowl with the remaining ingredients and toss until the potatoes are well coated,
- Place half the potatoes in your air fryer and place the metal holder in your air fryer. Place the remaining potatoes on the holder and cook for 25-30 minutes. Make sure to shake the basket about every 5 minutes.
- Toss the chips into a large bowl and sprinkle on the parmesan cheese.
- Allow the chips to cool for a few minutes before serving.

By Alicia Patterson

# Fried Green Tomatoes with Sriracha Mayonnaise Dipping Sauce

Prep Time: 15 Minutes / Cook Time: 16 Minutes / Servings: 4
Use the Steel Metal Holder

## INGREDIENTS FOR MAKING THIS RECIPE:

3 green tomatoes
salt and freshly ground black pepper
⅓ cup flour
2 eggs
½ cup buttermilk
1 cup panko breadcrumbs
1 cup cornmeal
fresh thyme sprigs or chopped fresh
chives

**Sriracha Mayo:**
½ cup mayonnaise
1 to 2 tablespoons Sriracha hot sauce
1 tablespoon milk

Olive oil spray

## DIRECTIONS FOR PREPARING THIS RECIPE:

- Spray the olive oil spray in the basket of your air fryer
- Preheat your air fryer to 320F.
- Slice the tomatoes into ¼ inch pieces. Use a paper towel to pat them dry. Salt and pepper to taste.
- Put the flour in a small bowl, mix together the buttermilk and eggs in another, mix together the cornmeal and breadcrumbs in a 3rd bowl.
- Dip the tomatoes in the flour, then buttermilk mixture, and finally the cornmeal mixture.
- Place ¼ of the tomatoes in your air fryer and then put in the metal holder. Place another ¼ of the tomatoes on the metal holder. Spray a little olive oil spray on top of the tomatoes. Cook for 8 minutes and flip the tomatoes halfway through spraying the tops again with olive oil spray. Repeat with remaining tomatoes.
- Mix together the Sriracha mayonnaise ingredients in a bowl while the tomatoes are cooking.
- Put the cooked tomatoes on a paper towel lined plate and allow them to cook for a few minutes.
- Serve the tomatoes with a side of the Sriracha mayonnaise.

Air Fryer Accessories Recipe Cookbook

# Roasted Chickpeas

Prep Time: 5 Minutes / Cook Time: 10 Minutes / Servings: 4
Use the Pizza Pan

## INGREDIENTS FOR MAKING THIS RECIPE:

*1 can chickpeas, drained and rinsed*
*1 tablespoon olive oil*
*Salt*
*Seasoning mix of your choice like za'atar, dirty rice, etc.*

## DIRECTIONS FOR PREPARING THIS RECIPE:

- Preheat your air fryer to 355F.
- Place the chickpeas in a bowl and toss with the olive oil. Salt to taste and add seasoning to taste. Toss again.
- Place the chickpeas in the pizza pan, put it in the basket of your preheated air fryer and set the timer for 8 minutes.
- Check the chickpeas and add an extra minute or 2 if not done to your liking.
- Place the cooked chickpeas in a bowl to serve.

By Alicia Patterson

# Plantain Chips

Prep Time: 5 Minutes/ Cook Time: 10 Minutes / Servings: 4

## INGREDIENTS FOR MAKING THIS RECIPE:

*1 Large plantain, pealed*
*1 teaspoon Coconut oil*
*1/4 teaspoon turmeric powder*
*1/2 teaspoon salt*
*Pinch chili powder*

## DIRECTIONS FOR PREPARING THIS RECIPE:

- Preheat your air fryer to 375F.
- Cut the plantain in small slices.
- Mix the plantain slices in a bowl with coconut oil salt, chili powder, and turmeric
- Place the plantain slices in the basket of your preheated air fryer and set the timer for 8 minutes. Shake the basket every 2 minutes.
- Place the cooked plantain chips in a bowl and let them rest for 2 minutes before serving.

Air Fryer Accessories Recipe Cookbook

# Buffalo Cauliflower

Prep Time: 5 Minutes/ Cook Time: 14 Minutes / Servings: 4
Use the Steel  Metal Holder

## INGREDIENTS FOR MAKING THIS RECIPE:

*1 medium head cauliflower, chopped into 1 1/2" florets (approximately 6 cups)*
*2-3 tablespoons Frank's Red Hot Sauce*
*1 1/2 teaspoons maple syrup*
*2 teaspoons avocado oil*
*2-3 tablespoons nutritional yeast*
*1/4 teaspoon sea salt*
*1 tablespoon cornstarch or arrowroot starch*

## DIRECTIONS FOR PREPARING THIS RECIPE:

- Preheat your air fryer to 360F.
- Whisk together all the ingredients except for the cauliflower in a bowl. Then toss the cauliflower in the mixture.
- Place half the cauliflower in the basket of your preheated air fryer and put the metal holder in it. Put the remaining cauliflower on it and set the timer for 14 minutes. Shake the basket Halfway through minutes. Remove and place the remaining cauliflower in the basket and cook for 10 minutes, shaking halfway through.
- Place the cooked cauliflower in a bowl to serving.

By Alicia Patterson

# Popcorn tofu with Sriracha Mayo

Prep Time: 15 Minutes / Cook Time: 12 Minutes / Servings: 4

## INGREDIENTS FOR MAKING THIS RECIPE:

*Popcorn Tofu:*
*14 oz extra firm tofu in water, water pressed out and drained*
*1/2 cup chickpea or quinoa flour*
*1/2 cup cornmeal*
*2 TB nutritional yeast*
*1 TB Better Than Bouillon Vegetarian No Chicken Base*
*1 TB Dijon mustard*
*1 teaspoon garlic powder*
*1 teaspoon onion powder*
*1/2 teaspoon salt*
*1/2 teaspoon pepper*
*3/4 cup unsweetened dairy free milk*
*1.5 cup panko bread crumbs gluten free if needed*

*Sriracha Mayo:*
*1/2 cup mayo*
*2 TB sriracha*

## DIRECTIONS FOR PREPARING THIS RECIPE:

* Preheat your air fryer to 350F.
* Mix the bouillon, garlic, salt, mustard, onion, pepper, yeast, milk, cornmeal and flower together in a large bowl. The mixture should have the same consistency as pancake batter. Add more milk if you need to thin it out.
* Put the panko in a separate bowl.
* Coat the tofu with the batter and then the panko.
* Place the tofu in the basket of your preheated air fryer and set the timer for 12 minutes. Shake the basket halfway through cooking process.
* While the tofu is cooking, mix together the mayo ingredients in a bowl.
* Serve the cooked tofu with a side of the sriracha mayo.

Air Fryer Accessories Recipe Cookbook

# Taco Matzo Chips

Prep Time: 5 Minutes / Cook Time: 8 Minutes / Servings: 4

## INGREDIENTS FOR MAKING THIS RECIPE:

5 sheets Matzo
1 ½ teaspoons Chili Powder
1 teaspoon Tomato Powder
1 teaspoon Sea Salt
1/4 teaspoon Garlic Powder
1/4 teaspoon Onion Powder
1/4 Tablespoon Paprika
1/4 teaspoon Ground Cumin
Tiny pinch Cayenne Pepper
1/4 cup Grated Parmesan Cheese
Olive oil spray

## DIRECTIONS FOR PREPARING THIS RECIPE:

* Grease the basket of your air fryer with olive oil spray and preheat your air fryer to 380F.
* Mix together everything but the matzo. Break the matzo into pieces that resemble tortilla chips. Then spray both side of the matzo with the olive oil spray.
* Put the matzo pieces in a bag along with the mixed ingredients. Seal the bag and shake it until the matzo is well coated.
* Place the matzo in the basket of your preheated air fryer and set the timer for 8 minutes.
* Place the browned matzo chips on a plate and allow them to cool before serving.

By Alicia Patterson

# Apple Chips

Prep Time: 10 Minutes / Cook Time: 15 Minutes / Servings: 2
Use the Pizza Pan

## INGREDIENTS FOR MAKING THIS RECIPE:

*1 apple, peeled, cored and thinly sliced horizontally*
*1/2 teaspoon. ground cinnamon*
*1 Tbs. sugar*
*Pinch of kosher salt*

## DIRECTIONS FOR PREPARING THIS RECIPE:

- Preheat your air fryer to 390F.
- Mix the cinnamon, salt and sugar together in a small bowl. Place the apple pieces on a baking sheet and evenly sprinkle the seasoning mix on them.
- Place half of the apple pieces in the basket of your preheated air fryer and set the timer for 8 minutes. Flip the pieces halfway through cooking. Repeat the same steps with the remaining apple pieces.
- Place the chips in a bowl and let them cool before serving.

Air Fryer Accessories Recipe Cookbook

# Patatas Bravas

Prep Time: 25 Minutes / Cook Time: 36 Minutes / Servings: 3-4
Use the Steel Metal Holder

## INGREDIENTS FOR MAKING THIS RECIPE:

10 ½ ounces red potatoes, cut into 1-inch chunks
1 tablespoon avocado oil, coconut oil, or peanut oil
1 teaspoon garlic powder
Pinch of sea salt & pepper

**Seasoning:**
1 tablespoon smoked paprika
1/2 teaspoon cayenne (optional)
Sea salt & pepper to taste

## DIRECTIONS FOR PREPARING THIS RECIPE:

- Bring water to a boil in a large pot. Add in the potatoes and allow them to cook for 6 minutes. Put the potatoes on a kitchen towel and pat them dry completely. Let the potatoes cool until their room temperature about 15 minutes.
- Towards the end of the cooling process, preheat your air fryer to 390F.
- Place the room temperature potatoes in a big bowl and toss with the garlic powder, oil and salt and pepper.
- Place half of the potatoes in the basket of your preheated air fryer and then put the metal holder in it. Place the other half of the potatoes on the metal holder and set the timer for 15 minutes. Shake the basket halfway through cooking. Repeat the same steps with the remaining potatoes.
- Put the cooked potatoes in a bowl and spray them with a little avocado or olive oil. Toss the potatoes with the seasoning until well coated.
- Serve Immediately.

By Alicia Patterson

# Fried Guacamole Balls

Prep Time: 6 Hours 15 Minutes / Cook Time: 8 Minutes / Servings: 2

## INGREDIENTS FOR MAKING THIS RECIPE:

Guacamole
3 medium ripe avocados
Juice from 1 lime
1/3 cup chopped onion
2 teaspoons cumin
Fresh finely chopped cilantro to taste, about 1/3 cup
Sea salt & pepper to taste
8 tablespoons fine almond flour

1 egg
1 egg white
1/3 cup almond flour
1 1/2 cups panko

## DIRECTIONS FOR PREPARING THIS RECIPE:

* Place all the guacamole ingredients in a bowl and mash them together until well mixed. Mix in the almond flour until the mixture reaches the consistency of brownie batter. Cover the bowl and place it in the freezer for 1 to 2 hours. You want the mixture to harden.
* Use parchment paper to line a baking sheet. Scoop out the guacamole and form 10 balls about the size of ping pongs balls. Place them on the baking sheet and freeze for at least 4 hours.
* Preheat your air fryer to 390F.
* Place the 1/3 cup almond flour in one dish, the panko in another, and beat the eggs together in another dish.
* Quickly spray the guacamole balls with olive oil. Coat them with almond flour then, egg, and finally panko.
* Place the ball in the basket of your preheated air fryer and set the timer for 8 minutes. The balls should be golden when done.
* Put the cooked balls on a plate to serve.

Air Fryer Accessories Recipe Cookbook

# Onion Roasted Potatoes

Prep Time: 5 Minutes / Cook Time: 15 Minutes / Servings: 4-6
Use the Pizza Pan

## INGREDIENTS FOR MAKING THIS RECIPE:

*2 lb. baby red potatoes*
*2 Tablespoon. olive oil*
*1 envelope Lipton onion soup mix*

## DIRECTIONS FOR PREPARING THIS RECIPE:

- Preheat your air fryer to 390F.
- Cut the potatoes into quarters and put them in a bowl.  Pout in the olive oil and toss until well coated. Pour in the onion soup mix and toss until well coated.
- Place the potatoes in the pizza pan and put in the basket of your preheated air fryer and set the timer for 17-20 minutes. Shake the basket halfway through cooking.
- Place the potatoes in a bowl and serve.

By Alicia Patterson

# Corn Tortilla Chips

Prep Time: 5 Minutes / Cook Time: 3 Minutes / Servings: 4
Use the Steel Metal Holder

## INGREDIENTS FOR MAKING THIS RECIPE:

*8 Corn Tortillas*
*1 tablespoon olive oil*
*Salt to taste*

## DIRECTIONS FOR PREPARING THIS RECIPE:

- Preheat your air fryer to 390F.
- Cut the tortillas into small triangular pieces.
- Brush or spray the pieces with olive oil
- Place half of the pieces on metal holder in the basket of your preheated air fryer and set the timer for 3 minutes. Repeat with the remaining pieces.
- Salt the cooked chips and serve.

# Parmesan Zucchini Chips

Prep Time: 10 Minutes / Cook Time: 8 Minutes / Servings: 4
Use the Pizza Pan

## INGREDIENTS FOR MAKING THIS RECIPE:

2 medium zucchinis, thinly sliced
1 egg
½ cup Italian breadcrumbs
½ cup grated parmesan
½ teaspoon smoked paprika
Cooking spray
Salt and pepper

## DIRECTIONS FOR PREPARING THIS RECIPE:

* Preheat your air fryer to 350F.
* Use paper towels to pat the zucchini dry.
* Lightly beat the eggs with a little water, and a little salt and pepper in a small bowl. Place the breadcrumbs in another bowl with the parmesan and paprika and mix them together.
* Coat the zucchini with the egg, and then the parmesan mixture. Then put them on a wire rack.
* Lightly spray the zucchini with cooking spray.
* Place the zucchini in a single layer in the basket of your preheated air fryer and set the timer for 8 minutes. Add a couple minutes if the chips aren't completely cooked.
* Add more salt and pepper to taste and serve.

By Alicia Patterson

# Broccoli with Cheese Sauce

Prep Time: 5 Minutes / Cook Time: 8 Minutes / Servings: 4

## INGREDIENTS FOR MAKING THIS RECIPE:

*6 cups broccoli florets (about 12 ounces)*
*Cooking spray*
*10 tablespoons low-fat evaporated milk*
*1 1/2 ounces queso fresco, crumbled (about 5 Tablespoons)*
*4 teaspoons aj amarillo paste*
*6 lower-sodium saltine crackers*

## DIRECTIONS FOR PREPARING THIS RECIPE:

- Preheat your air fryer to375F.
- Spray the broccoli with cooking spray until it's well coated.
- Place the broccoli in the basket of your air fryer, and the timer for 6 to 8 minutes. Shake the basket about halfway through cooking.
- While the broccoli is cooking, place all the remaining ingredients in a blender or food processor. Blend until the mixture becomes smooth, around 45 seconds.
- Put the mixture into a microwave safe bowl and microwave the mixture for around 30 seconds on high. The sauce should be warm when reading.
- Place the cooked broccoli on a bowl and top with the warm broccoli sauce to serve. Alternatively you can serve the cheese sauce in a bowl for dipping, so you can have more cheese sauce.

# Eggs

By Alicia Patterson

# Hard Boiled Eggs

Prep Time: 0 Minutes / Cook Time: 16 Minutes / Servings: 6 eggs

## INGREDIENTS FOR MAKING THIS RECIPE:

*6 eggs*
*Salt*

## DIRECTIONS FOR PREPARING THIS RECIPE:

* Place a small wire rack in the basket of your air fryer and preheat the air fryer to 250F.
* Put the eggs on the wire rack and set the timer for 16 minutes.
* While the eggs are cooking prepare an ice bath.
* Place the cooked eggs in the ice bath for a few minutes
* Peel and add salt to taste

Air Fryer Accessories Recipe Cookbook

# Two Egg Omelet

Prep Time: 10 Minutes / Cook Time: 10 Minutes / Servings: 1
Use the Pizza Pan

## INGREDIENTS FOR MAKING THIS RECIPE:

2 eggs
1/4 cup milk
Pinch of salt
Fresh meat and vegetables, diced
1 teaspoon McCormick Good Morning Breakfast Seasoning, Garden Herb
1/4 cup shredded cheese

## DIRECTIONS FOR PREPARING THIS RECIPE:

- Preheat your air fryer to 350F.
- Combine the milk and eggs in a bowl and mix well. Add the salt.
- Mix in the meat and vegetables until well combined.
- Pour the mixture into the pizza pan.
- Put the pan in the basket of your preheated air fryer and cook for 8 to 10 minutes.
- When the omelet is halfway through the cooking process season with the McCormick seasoning and top with cheese.
- Use a spatula to get the sides of the omelet loose from the pan. Place the omelet on a plate to serve.

By Alicia Patterson

# Fried Eggs

Prep Time: 0 Minutes / Cook Time: 3 Minutes / Servings: 1

## INGREDIENTS FOR MAKING THIS RECIPE:

*2 eggs*
*Salt and pepper*
*Hot sauce (optional)*

## DIRECTIONS FOR PREPARING THIS RECIPE:

- Place a 6x3 pan in the basket of your air fryer and preheat your air fryer to 370F.
- Crack the eggs directly into the pan in your air fryer and set the timer for 3 minutes.
- Check on the eggs after the 3 minutes and add an additional minute if you like your eggs more done.
- Place the cooked eggs on a plate and add salt, pepper, and hot sauce to taste.

Air Fryer Accessories Recipe Cookbook

# Shirred Eggs

Prep Time: 5 Minutes / Cook Time: 12 Minutes / Servings: 1

## INGREDIENTS FOR MAKING THIS RECIPE:

2 teaspoons unsalted butter, at room temperature
2 thin slices Black Forest ham, about 1½ - 2 ounces total
4 large eggs
2 tablespoons heavy cream
¾ teaspoon kosher salt
¼ teaspoon ground black pepper
3 tablespoons finely grated Parmesan cheese
⅛ teaspoon Pimenton or smoked paprika
2 teaspoons chopped fresh chives
Toasted bread, for serving

## DIRECTIONS FOR PREPARING THIS RECIPE:

- Preheat your air fryer to 320F and grease a pie tin with butter.
- Place 1 egg, ¼ teaspoon salt, half the pepper, and cream in a small bowl and mix them together using a whisk.
- Put the ham in the pie tin and pour the egg mixture on top of it. Put in the remaining eggs, and season with salt and pepper, and the parmesan.
- Place the pie tin in the basket of your air fryer and set the timer for 12 minutes.
- Season the cooked eggs with the paprika, and top with chives.
- Use a spatula to carefully remove the dish from the tin and place it on a plate.
- Serve immediately with a side of toast.

By Alicia Patterson

# Soft Boiled Eggs

Prep Time: 10 Minutes / Cook Time: 8 Minutes / Servings: 6 eggs

## INGREDIENTS FOR MAKING THIS RECIPE:

*6 eggs*
*Salt*

## DIRECTIONS FOR PREPARING THIS RECIPE:

* Preheat the air fryer to 250F.
* Put the eggs on the wire rack and set the timer for 8 minutes.
* While the eggs are cooking prepare an ice bath.
* Place the cooked eggs in the ice bath for about 10 minutes
* Peel and add salt to taste.

Air Fryer Accessories Recipe Cookbook

# Baked Eggs

Prep Time: 10 Minutes / Cook Time: 8 Minutes / Servings: 2 eggs

## INGREDIENTS FOR MAKING THIS RECIPE:

*2 eggs*
*Non-stick cooking spray*
*Salt*

## DIRECTIONS FOR PREPARING THIS RECIPE:

- Preheat the air fryer to 180F.
- Generously spray 2 ramekins with non-stick cooking spray
- Crack 1 egg into each ramekin
- Place the ramekins in the basket of your preheated air fryer, raise the temperature to 330F, and set the timer for minutes.
- Salt the cooked eggs to taste and eat the eggs directly out of the ramekins, or use a spatula to loosen the sides, and place on a plate.

By Alicia Patterson

# Eggs In A Mini Bread Bowl

Prep Time: 15 Minutes / Cook Time: 25 Minutes / Servings: 4

## INGREDIENTS FOR MAKING THIS RECIPE:

*4 crusty dinner rolls*
*4 eggs, large*
*4 tablespoons mixed herbs such as parsley, chives, tarragon, chopped*
*4 tablespoons heavy cream*
*Salt and pepper*
*Parmesan cheese, grated*

## DIRECTIONS FOR PREPARING THIS RECIPE:

- Preheat the air fryer to 350F.
- Cut the tops off the rolls and remove enough of the inside to add in an egg.
- Crack 1 egg into each dinner roll.
- Top each egg with 1 tablespoon of the herb, 1 tablespoon of the cream. Add salt and pepper to taste, and sprinkle with parmesan to taste.
- Place the rolls in your preheated air fryer and set the timer for 25 minutes.
- Let the cooked rolls rest for 5 minutes.
- Place the bread tops back on the rolls to serve.

Air Fryer Accessories Recipe Cookbook

# Scrambled Eggs

Prep Time: 3 Minutes / Cook Time: 25 Minutes / Servings: 1

## INGREDIENTS FOR MAKING THIS RECIPE:

*2 eggs*
*Salt and pepper*
*1 tablespoon butter*

## DIRECTIONS FOR PREPARING THIS RECIPE:

- Place a 6x3 pan in the basket of your air fryer, add a tablespoon of butter to the pan, and preheat the air fryer at 220F for 1 minute.
- While the air fryer is preheating, mix all the remaining ingredients in a small bowl.
- Pour the mixture into the pan in the basket in your air fryer and set the timer for 2 minutes.
- After the 2 minutes, use a fork to scrape the pan and continue to cook in 2 minute intervals until desire doneness is reached.
- Place the cooked eggs on a plate to serve.

By Alicia Patterson

# Breakfast Soufflé

Prep Time: 5 Minutes / Cook Time: 8 Minutes / Servings: 2

## INGREDIENTS FOR MAKING THIS RECIPE:

*2 eggs*
*2 tablespoons (light) cream*
*Red chili pepper*
*Parsley*

## DIRECTIONS FOR PREPARING THIS RECIPE:

* Preheat your air fryer to 200F.
* Finely chop the parsley and mix it with the remaining ingredients in a small bowl.
* Fill 2 ramekins halfway with the mixture.
* Place the ramekins in the basket of your preheated air fryer and set the timer for 8 minutes.
* Serve the cooked soufflés immediately.

Air Fryer Accessories Recipe Cookbook

# Scotch Eggs

Prep Time: 5 Minutes / Cook Time: 8 Minutes / Servings: 2

## INGREDIENTS FOR MAKING THIS RECIPE:

1/3 cup finely chopped onion
1 tablespoon snipped fresh chives
1 clove garlic, minced
1 teaspoon snipped fresh thyme
1 teaspoon salt
1 teaspoon pepper
½ teaspoon snipped fresh sage
1 lb. ground pork
½ cup all-purpose flour
½ teaspoon smoked paprika (optional)
2 eggs

2 tablespoons water
1 ½ cups panko bread crumbs
6 eggs, hard-cooked or soft-boiled, peeled
6 cups arugula or fresh spinach

**Sauce:**
½ cup mayonnaise
1 – 2 tablespoons Sriracha sauce
2 teaspoons lemon juice
1 clove garlic, minced

## DIRECTIONS FOR PREPARING THIS RECIPE:

* Preheat your air fryer to 350F.
* Mix the garlic, chives, sage, onion, ½ teaspoon salt, half teaspoon pepper, and thyme together in a medium bowl. Put in the pork and mix until everything is well combined.
* Mix the remaining salt and pepper, flour, and paprika in a shallow dish.
* Beat together the eggs in and water in a different dish. Put the panko in another dish.
* Separate the pork mixture into 6 equal portions and form them into patties.
* Dip the cooked eggs in the flour mixture and mold the pork patties around the eggs. Make sure the eggs are fully coated with the pork.
* Dip each egg in the flour mixture again one by one. Remove any extra flour by shaking the eggs. Dip the eggs in the beaten egg mixture, and then coat them with the panko.
* Put the eggs in the basket of your preheated air fryer and set the timer for 15 minutes.
* While the eggs are cooking, mix together all the sauce ingredients in a bowl.
* Place the arugula on 6 plates. Place 1 egg on each plate and drizzle with the sauce.
* Serve immediately.

By Alicia Patterson

# Ham and Eggs Toast Cups

Prep Time: 10 Minutes / Cook Time: 15 Minutes / Servings: 4

## INGREDIENTS FOR MAKING THIS RECIPE:

*4 Eggs*
*8 Slices of Toast*
*2 Slices of Ham*
*Butter*
*Salt*
*Pepper*
*Cheese (Optional)*

## DIRECTIONS FOR PREPARING THIS RECIPE:

* Preheat your air fryer to 160F.
* Grease 4 ramekins with butter.
* Use your hand or a rolling pin to flatten the toast as much as possible.
* Use 1 piece of bread to line each ramekin. Then top the bread with a second slice of bread. Make sure the entire interior of the ramekin is covered with bread. Flatten the bread out as much as possible.
* Cut the ham into 8 equal size pieces. Line the bread in the ramekin with 2 slices of ham creating a circle in the middle of the two pieces of ham. Crack an egg into the circle created by the ham in each ramekin. Add salt and pepper to taste to the egg, and top with cheese.
* Place the ramekins in the basket of your preheated air fryer and set the timer for 15 minutes.
* Use a knife to free the sides of the toast from the ramekin and then use the knife to gently remove the cups. Serve immediately.

Air Fryer Accessories Recipe Cookbook

# Chorizo and Potato Frittata

Prep Time: 10 Minutes / Cook Time: 15 Minutes / Servings: 4
Use the Pizza Pan

## INGREDIENTS FOR MAKING THIS RECIPE:

3 jumbo free-range eggs
½ chorizo sausage, sliced
1 big potato, par-boiled and cubed
½ cup frozen corn
olive oil
chopped parsley
½ wheel of feta
salt/pepper

## DIRECTIONS FOR PREPARING THIS RECIPE:

- Place a good tablespoon or 2 of olive oil in the pizza pan along with the corn, chorizo, and potato and place it in the basket of your air fryer. Set the temperature to 355F and the timer for 4 minutes. After the 4 minutes check the potatoes and chorizo. Keep on adding time in 2 minute intervals until they're browned.
- While the ingredients are cooking, beat the eggs. Add salt and pepper to taste.
- Pour the eggs into the basket of your air fryer along with the feta and parsley, and set the timer for 5 minutes.
- Place the cooked frittata on a plate to serve.

By Alicia Patterson

# Spinach and Sausage Egg Cups

Prep Time: 10 Minutes / Cook Time: 10 Minutes / Servings: 3

## INGREDIENTS FOR MAKING THIS RECIPE:

6 tablespoons sausage, cooked & crumbled
6 tablespoons frozen chopped spinach
6 teaspoons shredded Co-Jack cheese
¼ cup Egg substitute

## DIRECTIONS FOR PREPARING THIS RECIPE:

- Preheat your air fryer to 330F.
- Place an equal amount of sausage in 6 silicone cupcake holders. Then place an equal amount of cheese in each and finally add in the egg substitute.
- Put the cupcake holders into the basket of your air fryer and set the timer for 10 minutes.

Air Fryer Accessories Recipe Cookbook

# Avocado Egg Cups

Prep Time: 10 Minutes / Cook Time: 10 Minutes / Servings: 2

## INGREDIENTS FOR MAKING THIS RECIPE:

*2 Medium Avocados*
*4 Small Eggs*
*Fresh Parsley*
*Fresh Chives*
*Salt & Pepper*

## DIRECTIONS FOR PREPARING THIS RECIPE:

- Preheat your air fryer to 345F.
- Cut the avocados in half and remove the pit. Scoop out about 20% of the flesh from both halves. Add chives, parsley, and salt and pepper to taste.
- Place an egg into the scooped out area of each avocado.
- Put the avocado halves into the basket of your air fryer and set the timer for 8 minutes.
- Add more salt and pepper, and parsley to taste before serving.

By Alicia Patterson

# Portobello and Parmesan Egg Cups

Prep Time: 10 Minutes / Cook Time: 10 Minutes / Servings: 2

## INGREDIENTS FOR MAKING THIS RECIPE:

2 medium Portobello mushrooms, stems removed and dark gills scraped out
2 teaspoons olive oil
2 large eggs
2 tablespoons grated parmesan
Chopped basil
Salt and pepper

## DIRECTIONS FOR PREPARING THIS RECIPE:

- Preheat your air fryer to 390F.
- Coat the mushrooms with oil using a brush. Add salt and pepper to taste.
- Place an egg into the scooped out area of each avocado.
- Put the Portobellos cut side up into the basket of your air fryer, crack 1 egg into the eggs, add then top with the parmesan. Set the timer for 10 to 14 minutes. The yolk and whites should be firm when cooked.
- Top with basil to serve.

Air Fryer Accessories Recipe Cookbook

# Breakfast

By Alicia Patterson

# Pancakes

Prep Time: 9 Minutes / Cook Time: 6 Minutes / Servings: 1
Use the Pizza Pan

## INGREDIENTS FOR MAKING THIS RECIPE:

1 1/2 cup flour
3 1/2 teaspoons baking powder
1 1/2 teaspoon baking soda
1 teaspoon salt
1 tablespoon sugar
1 1/4 cups milk
1 egg
3 tablespoons melted butter

## DIRECTIONS FOR PREPARING THIS RECIPE:

* Preheat your air fryer to 220F.
* Place all the ingredients in a big bowl and use a whisk to mix them together.
* Let the mixture sit for 4 minutes.
* Coat the pizza pan with cooking spray.
* Pour the batter into the pan in the thinnest layer possible.
* Place the pan in the basket of your preheated air fryer and set the timer for 3 minutes.
* Check the pancake and keep on cooking in 3 minute intervals until cooked.
* Serve immediately.

Air Fryer Accessories Recipe Cookbook

# German Pancakes

Prep Time: 5 Minutes / Cook Time: 8 Minutes / Servings: 5

## INGREDIENTS FOR MAKING THIS RECIPE:

*3 whole eggs*
*1 cup whole wheat flour*
*Substitutes: oat flour*
*1 cup almond milk*
*Pinch of salt*
*2 heaping tablespoons unsweetened applesauce*

## DIRECTIONS FOR PREPARING THIS RECIPE:

- Preheat your air fryer to 390F.
- Put all the ingredients in a food processor or blender and blend until the mixture turns into a smooth batter.
- Pour a ½ cup of the batter in a small cast iron tray or ramekin.
- Place the tray or ramekin in the basket of your preheated air fryer and set the timer for 6 to 8 minutes. Repeat the process with the remaining batter.
- Serve immediately and garnish with your favorite berries or other fruit.

By Alicia Patterson

# French Toast Sticks

Prep Time: 5 Minutes / Cook Time: 10 Minutes / Servings: 5

## INGREDIENTS FOR MAKING THIS RECIPE:

*4 Slices Whole Wheat Bread*
*2 Large Eggs*
*¼ Cup Whole Milk*
*¼ Cup Brown Sugar*
*1 Tablespoon Honey*
*1 Teaspoon Cinnamon*
*Pinch of Nutmeg*
*Pinch of Icing Sugar*

## DIRECTIONS FOR PREPARING THIS RECIPE:

- Preheat your air fryer to 320F.
- Cut each piece of bread into 4 pieces
- Mix all the remaining ingredients except for the icing sugar together in a medium bowl.
- Dip the pieces of bread in the mixture until well coated.
- Place the bread pieces in the basket of your preheated air fryer and set the timer for 10 minutes. Flip the bread halfway through.
- Garnish the French sticks with icing sugar and serve immediately.

Air Fryer Accessories Recipe Cookbook

# Lemon Blueberry Muffins

Prep Time: 8 Minutes / Cook Time: 12 Minutes / Servings: 12
Use The Mini Cake Silicone Pan

## INGREDIENTS FOR MAKING THIS RECIPE:

2 1/2 cups self rising flour
1/2 cup Monk Fruit (or use your preferred sugar)
1/2 cup cream
1/4 cup avocado oil (any light cooking oil)
2 eggs
1 cup blueberries
Zest from 1 lemon
Juice from 1 lemon
1 teaspoon vanilla
Brown sugar for topping

## DIRECTIONS FOR PREPARING THIS RECIPE:

* Preheat your air fryer to 320F.
* Mix the flour and sugar together in a small bowl.
* Mix the cream, vanilla, eggs, oil, and lemon juice in a medium bowl.
* Pour the sugar mixture into the cream mixture and stir until just blended.
* Pour the mixture into mini cake pan. Top each cupcake holder with ½ teaspoon brown sugar.
* Place the mini cake pan in the basket of your preheated air fryer and set the timer for 10 minutes. Check on the muffins at the 6 minute mark. The muffins are cooked when a toothpick is inserted in the middle and comes out clean. Repeat with any remaining batter.
* Allow the muffins to cool for a few minute before serving.

By Alicia Patterson

# Cinnamon Crumb Coffee Cake Muffins

Prep Time: 7 Minutes / Cook Time: 20 Minutes / Servings: 8

## INGREDIENTS FOR MAKING THIS RECIPE:

*Muffin Batter*
*1 cup AP flour*
*1 1/4 teaspoon baking powder*
*1/4 teaspoon salt*
*1/2 cup granulated Monk Fruit (or use your preferred sugar substitute)*
*1 large egg, room temperature*
*1/2 cup buttermilk*
*2 1/2 tablespoons unsalted butter, melted & cooled*
*1 teaspoon. vanilla extract*

*Crumb Topping:*
*2/3 cup flour*
*1/3 cup coconut sugar*
*1 teaspoon ground cinnamon*
*1/8 teaspoon salt*
*1/4 cup butter, melted & cooled*

## DIRECTIONS FOR PREPARING THIS RECIPE:

- Preheat your air fryer to 360F.
- Mix the flour, salt, and baking soda together in a medium bowl.
- Mix the buttermilk, vanilla, eggs, sugar, and butter in a separate bowl.
- Pour the buttermilk mix into the baking soda mixture. Stir until just blended.
- Pour the mixture into silicone cupcake holders.
- Place the topping ingredients except for the butter in the same medium bowl (just used) Use a wooden spoon to stir in the butter until a crumb mixture is created.
- Top the cupcake holders with the crumb mixture
- Place the cupcake holder in the basket of your preheated air fryer. Set timer for 15 min. Check on the muffins at the 15 min mark. The muffins are cooked when a toothpick is inserted in the middle and comes out clean.
- Allow the muffins to cool on a wire rack for a few minutes before serving.

Air Fryer Accessories Recipe Cookbook

# Potato and Tofu Scramble

Prep Time: 5 Minutes / Cook Time: 30 Minutes / Servings: 3

## INGREDIENTS FOR MAKING THIS RECIPE:

1 block tofu chopped into 1" pieces
2 tablespoons soy sauce
1 tablespoon olive oil
1 teaspoon turmeric
1/2 teaspoon garlic powder
1/2 teaspoon onion powder
1/2 cup chopped onion

2 1/2 cups chopped red potato 1" cubes, 2-3 potatoes
1 tablespoon olive oil

4 cups broccoli florets

## DIRECTIONS FOR PREPARING THIS RECIPE:

- Preheat your air fryer to 400F.
- Put the soy sauce, onion powder, garlic powder, turmeric, onions, and olive oil in a bowl. Add in the tofu and toss until well combined.
- Toss the potatoes in a separate small bowl with 1 tablespoon olive oil.
- Place the potatoes in your preheated air fryer and set the timer for 15 minutes. Shake the basket halfway through.
- When the 15 minutes is up, shake the basket again, add in the tofu, and save any excess marinade. Lower the air fryer to 370F and set the timer for 15 minutes.
- While the mixture is cooking, mix the broccoli with the excess marinade. Add a little more soy sauce if there isn't enough liquid to coat the broccoli. Put the broccoli in the air fryer when there's 5 minutes left in the cooking process.
- Place the cooked mixture on a plate to serve.

By Alicia Patterson

# French Toast

Prep Time: 5 Minutes / Cook Time: 6 Minutes / Servings: 2

## INGREDIENTS FOR MAKING THIS RECIPE:

*4 slices of bread*
*2 eggs*
*⅔ cup of milk*
*1 teaspoon of vanilla*
*1 tablespoon of cinnamon*

## DIRECTIONS FOR PREPARING THIS RECIPE:

- Preheat your air fryer to 320F.
- Place all ingredient except for the bread in a medium bowl and use a fork to mix them together. Make sure everything is well combined and toe egg is broken up.
- Dip the bread in the liquid mixture and shake off any extra liquid.
- Spray an air fryer safe pan with cooking spray and place the bread in the pan
- Place the pan in the basket of your preheated air fryer and set the timer for 6 minutes. Flip the bread halfway through
- Serve immediately.

Air Fryer Accessories Recipe Cookbook

# Paleo Pumpkin Muffins

Prep Time: 9 Minutes / Cook Time: 6 Minutes / Servings: 12
Use The Mini Cake Silicone Pan

## INGREDIENTS FOR MAKING THIS RECIPE:

1 Cup Pumpkin Puree
2 Cups Gluten Free Oats
½ Cup Honey
2 Medium Eggs beaten
1 Teaspoon Coconut Butter
1 Tablespoon Cocoa Nibs
1 Tablespoon Vanilla Essence
1 Teaspoon Nutmeg

## DIRECTIONS FOR PREPARING THIS RECIPE:

- Preheat your air fryer to 355F.
- Put all the ingredients in a food processor or blender and blend until completely smooth.
- Place the batter in the silicone mini cake pan.
- Place the mini cake pan in the basket of your preheated air fryer and set the timer for 15 minutes. Repeat with the remaining batter.
- Allow the muffins to cool before serving.

By Alicia Patterson

# Easy Donuts

Prep Time: 9 Minutes / Cook Time: 6 Minutes / Servings: 6
Use the Steel Metal Holder

## INGREDIENTS FOR MAKING THIS RECIPE:

*1 can flaky pre-made biscuit dough*
*1/2 cup white sugar*
*1 teaspoon cinnamon*
*Coconut oil*
*Melted butter*

## DIRECTIONS FOR PREPARING THIS RECIPE:

- Spray the basket of your air fryer with cooking spray and preheat it to 350F.
- Separate the dough into individual biscuits. Cut a hole in the center of each donut with a shot glass or biscuit cutter.
- Place half the dough in your preheated air fryer and then the metal holder. Place the remaining dough on the metal holder and set the timer for 4 to 5 minutes.
- Mix the cinnamon and sugar together in a bowl.
- Use a brush to coat the cooked donuts with the melted butter.
- Coat the donuts with the cinnamon and sugar mixture.
- Allow the donuts to cool for a couple minutes before serving.

Air Fryer Accessories Recipe Cookbook

# Baked Oatmeal

Prep Time: 8 Minutes / Cook Time: 10 Minutes / Servings: 1

## INGREDIENTS FOR MAKING THIS RECIPE:

1 cup of milk
1 egg
2 cup of mixed berries, divided
1 cup of rolled oats
½ teaspoon of baking powder
½ teaspoon of ground cinnamon
⅓ teaspoon of salt
⅙ cup of brown sugar
⅛ cup of slivered almonds

## DIRECTIONS FOR PREPARING THIS RECIPE:

- Preheat the air fryer to 320F. Coat an air fryer safe pan with cooking spray.
- Mix the milk and egg together in a bowl.
- Mix the baking powder, oats, brown sugar, salt, and cinnamon in a medium bowl.
- Put ¼ cup of fruit in the pan, then the oat and brown sugar mixture, and finally the milk mixture.
- Allow the mixture to rest for 10 minutes then top with more fruit. Season with nutmeg and add the almonds.
- Place the pan in the basket of your preheated air fryer and set the timer for 10 minutes. Check the oats after 10 minutes and cook for a couple more minutes if necessary.
- Allow the oats to cool for a couple minutes before serving.

By Alicia Patterson

# Dessert

Air Fryer Accessories Recipe Cookbook

# Apple Fries with Whip Cream Caramel Sauce

Prep Time: 15 Minutes / Cook Time: 15 Minutes / Servings: 6
Use the Steel Metal Holder

## INGREDIENTS FOR MAKING THIS RECIPE:

3 Pink Lady or Honeycrisp apples, peeled, cored and cut into 8 wedges
½ cup flour
3 eggs, beaten
1 cup graham cracker crumbs
¼ cup sugar
8 ounces whipped cream cheese
½ cup caramel sauce, plus more for garnish
Cooking spray

## DIRECTIONS FOR PREPARING THIS RECIPE:

- Spray the basket of your air fryer and metal holder with cooking spray.
- Preheat your air fryer to 380F. Place the eggs in a small bowl, and mix the sugar and graham cracker in a small bowl.
- Place half the apple slices in your air fryer and then the metal hold. Place the remaining apple slices on the metal holder and cook for 7 minutes. Flip the apples after 5 minutes.
- While the apples are cooking, mix together the cream cheese and caramel sauce in a bowl, until well combined. Make a fun design in top with more caramel sauce.
- Serve the cooked apples with the caramel sauce.

By Alicia Patterson

# Peanut Butter and Banana Bites

Prep Time: 15 Minutes / Cook Time: 15 Minutes / Servings: 6

## INGREDIENTS FOR MAKING THIS RECIPE:

3 Pink Lady or Honeycrisp apples, peeled, cored and cut into 8 wedges
½ cup flour
3 eggs, beaten
1 cup graham cracker crumbs
¼ cup sugar
8 ounces whipped cream cheese
½ cup caramel sauce, plus more for garnish
Olive oil spray
A little lemon juice

## DIRECTIONS FOR PREPARING THIS RECIPE:

- Preheat your air fryer to 380.
- Put water in a bowl and add a little lemon juice. Cut the banana in slices and place the slices in the water.
- Place 1 slice of banana in the center of one of the wonton wrappers. Top the banana slice with 1 teaspoon of peanut butter.
- Use a brush to coat the edges of the wonton with water. Bring 2 opposite sides of the wonton together and squeeze. Do the same with the remaining side. Repeat the process with the remaining banana slices.
- Place the wontons in your air fryer and spray with olive oil spray. Cook the bites for 6 minutes.
- Serve the bites with a side of vanilla ice cream.

Air Fryer Accessories Recipe Cookbook

# Nutella and Banana Sandwiches

Prep Time: 5 Minutes / Cook Time: 15 Minutes / Servings: 2

## INGREDIENTS FOR MAKING THIS RECIPE:

*butter, softened*
*4 slices white bread*
*¼ cup chocolate hazelnut spread (Nutella®)*
*1 banana*

## DIRECTIONS FOR PREPARING THIS RECIPE:

- Preheat your air fryer to 370.
- Cut the banana into 6 pieces. Spread the chocolate spread on 1 side of each piece of bread. Place 3 pieces of banana on top of the Nutella on 2 pieces of bread. Top with the Nutella side of the remaining bread. Spread the butter on the other side of all 4 pieces of bread. Cut the sandwiches in half.
- Place the sandwiches in your air fryer and cook for 8 minutes. Flip the sandwiches after 5 minutes.
- Serve the hot sandwiches immediately with a glass of milk.

By Alicia Patterson

# Double Chocolate Brownies

Prep Time: 10 Minutes / Cook Time: 20 Minutes / Servings: 4
Use the Cake Pan or Mini Cake Silicone Pan

## INGREDIENTS FOR MAKING THIS RECIPE:

### DRY  INGREDIENTS FOR MAKING THIS RECIPE:
1/2 cup whole wheat pastry flour
1/2 cup sugar
1/4 cup cocoa powder
1 tablespoon ground flax seeds
1/4 teaspoon salt

### WET  INGREDIENTS FOR MAKING THIS RECIPE:
1/4 cup non-dairy milk
1/4 cup aquafaba
1/2 teaspoon vanilla extract

### MIX-INS:
1/4 cup chocolate chips or mix-in of your choice
Cooking spray

## DIRECTIONS FOR PREPARING THIS RECIPE:

- Preheat your air fryer to 350.
- Combine the wet ingredients together in a small bowl. Combine the dry ingredients together in a medium bowl.
- Pour the wet ingredients into the dry ingredient and combine well. Pour in the mix-ins and combine again.
- Spray the cake pan with cooking spray and pour the mixture into it.
- Put the pan in your air fryer and cook for 20 minutes. If the center is not fully cooked after 20 minutes, cook for an additional 5 minutes.
- Allow the brownies to cool for a few minutes before serving

Air Fryer Accessories Recipe Cookbook

# Caramel Popcorn

Prep Time: 5 Minutes / Cook Time: 15 Minutes / Servings: 6

## INGREDIENTS FOR MAKING THIS RECIPE:

*3 tablespoons dried corn kernels*
*spray avocado oil, coconut oil, safflower oil, or peanut oil*
*salt to taste*

*Caramel:*
*1/2 Cup Butter, Sweet Cream Salted*
*1/2 Cup Light Brown Sugar*
*1 tsp Vanilla*
*1/4 tsp Baking Soda*

## DIRECTIONS FOR PREPARING THIS RECIPE:

- Line the sides of the air fryer basket with aluminum foil and preheat your air fryer to 390F. Line a baking sheet with aluminum foil
- Place the corn kernels in the basket of your preheated air fryer, spray them with the oil and set the timer for 15 minutes. Stay close because the popcorn could finish sooner. If the popping stops the popcorn is cooked.
- Place the popcorn in a big bowl and salt to taste.
- Place the butter in a medium saucepan and heat it on medium heat until it melts.
- Mix in the brown sugar
- Keep stirring the mixture as it comes to a boil.
- Stop stirring the boiling mixture and let it cook for 5 minutes.
- After 4 minutes add the vanilla and stir. After the 5 minutes it's done add the baking soda.
- Pour the caramel sauce over the popcorn and use a spoon to combine the mixture until the popcorn is coated with caramel.
- Let the caramel corn on the aluminum foil lined baking sheet to cool
- Serve the popcorn once it's cooled.

By Alicia Patterson

# Banana Churro

Prep Time: 10 Minutes / Cook Time: 20 Minutes / Servings: 3
Use the Cake Pan or Mini Cake Silicone Pan

## INGREDIENTS FOR MAKING THIS RECIPE:

*2 Large Bananas*
*1/2 Cup Flour*
*a pinch of salt*
*2 Eggs, whisked*
*3/4 Cup Bread Crumbs*
*Cinnamon Sugar*
*Olive Oil*

## DIRECTIONS FOR PREPARING THIS RECIPE:

- Preheat your air fryer to 355.
- Cut each banana into 3 pieces
- Mix the flour and salt together in one bowl, place the eggs in another, the breadcrumbs in a 3rd bowl, and the cinnamon sugar in a 4th.
- Dip the bananas in the flour, then egg, then finally breadcrumbs.
- Place a small amount of olive oil in another bowl and lightly coat the bananas with it.
- Place the bananas in your air fryer in 2 batches and cook for 8 minutes. Shake the basket halfway through.
- Roll the cooked bananas in the cinnamon sugar and serve.

Air Fryer Accessories Recipe Cookbook

# Popcorn

Prep Time: 5 Minutes / Cook Time: 15 Minutes / Servings: 6

## INGREDIENTS FOR MAKING THIS RECIPE:

*3 tablespoons dried corn kernels*
*Spray avocado oil, coconut oil, safflower oil, or peanut oil*
*Salt & pepper to taste*

## DIRECTIONS FOR PREPARING THIS RECIPE:

- Line the sides of the air fryer basket with aluminum foil and preheat your air fryer to 390F.
- Place the corn kernels in the basket of your preheated air fryer, spray them with the oil and set the timer for 15 minutes. Stay close because the popcorn could finish sooner. If the popping sound stops the popcorn is cooked.
- Place the popcorn in a big bowl, spray with a little more oil, and add salt and pepper to taste.
- Serve immediately.

By Alicia Patterson

# Caramel Popcorn

Prep Time: 5 Minutes / Cook Time: 15 Minutes / Servings: 6

## INGREDIENTS FOR MAKING THIS RECIPE:

*3 tablespoons dried corn kernels*
*Spray avocado oil, coconut oil, safflower oil, or peanut oil*
*Salt to taste*

*Caramel:*
*1/2 Cup Butter, Sweet Cream Salted*
*1/2 Cup Light Brown Sugar*
*1 teaspoon Vanilla*
*1/4 teaspoon Baking Soda*

## DIRECTIONS FOR PREPARING THIS RECIPE:

- Line the sides of the air fryer basket with aluminum foil and preheat your air fryer to 390F. Line a baking sheet with aluminum foil
- Place the corn kernels in the basket of your preheated air fryer, spray them with the oil and set the timer for 15 minutes. Stay close because the popcorn could finish sooner. If the popping sound stops the popcorn is cooked.
- Place the popcorn in a big bowl and salt to taste.
- Place the butter in a medium saucepan and heat it on medium heat until it melts.
- Mix in the brown sugar
- Keep stirring the mixture as it comes to a boil.
- Stop stirring the boiling mixture and let it cook for 5 minutes.
- After 4 minutes add the vanilla and stir. After the 5 minutes it's done add the baking soda.
- Pour the caramel sauce over the popcorn and use a spoon to combine the mixture until the popcorn is coated with caramel.
- Place the caramel corn on the aluminum foil lined baking sheet to cool
- Serve the popcorn once it's cooled.

Air Fryer Accessories Recipe Cookbook

# Apple Dumplings

Prep Time: 15 Minutes / Cook Time: 25 Minutes / Servings: 2

## INGREDIENTS FOR MAKING THIS RECIPE:

*2 very small apples, cored and peeled*
*2 tablespoons raisins or sultanas*
*1 tablespoon brown sugar*
*2 sheets puff pastry*
*2 tablespoons butter, melted*

## DIRECTIONS FOR PREPARING THIS RECIPE:

- Preheat your air fryer to 356F.
- Combine the brown sugar and sultanas or raisins in a bowl.
- Place each apple on a puff pastry sheet. Put some of the brown sugar mixture in the area where the core was in each apple.
- Fold the pastry up over the apple and cover it completely.
- Use a brush to coat the pastry with melted butter.
- Place aluminum foil in the basket of your preheated air fryer, place the pastries on top of it, and set the timer for 25 minutes. Flip the pastries about halfway through.
- Allow the cooked dumplings to cool for about 10 minutes before serving.

By Alicia Patterson

# Fruit Crumble Mug Cake

Prep Time: 15 Minutes / Cook Time: 15 Minutes / Servings: 4

## INGREDIENTS FOR MAKING THIS RECIPE:

*110 g Plain Flour*
*50 g Butter*
*30 g Caster Sugar*
*30 g Gluten Free Oats*
*25 g Brown Sugar*
*4 Plums*
*1 Small Apple*
*1 Small Pear*
*1 Small Peach*
*Handful Blueberries*
*1 Tablespoon Honey*

## DIRECTIONS FOR PREPARING THIS RECIPE:

- Preheat your air fryer to 320F.
- Take out the stones and cores from all of the fruit. Slice the fruit in small square chunks.
- Divide the fruit between 4 mugs. Top with enough honey and brown sugar to cover the fruit.
- Mix the butter, caster sugar, and flour in a bowl until the mixture looks like small breadcrumbs. Then mix in the oats.
- Place the mixture on top of the fruit in each mug.
- Place the mugs in the basket of your preheated air fryer, and set the timer for 10 minutes. After the ten minutes are up, raise the temperature to 390F and cook for an additional 5 minutes.
- Serve immediately.

Air Fryer Accessories Recipe Cookbook

# Chocolate Cake

Prep Time: 10 Minutes / Cook Time: 45 Minutes / Servings: 6-8
Use the Cake Pan (Use Mini Cake Silicone Pan for Mini Cupcakes)

## INGREDIENTS FOR MAKING THIS RECIPE:

*180 g Brown Sugar*
*109 g All-purpose Flour*
*60 g Unsweetened Cocoa Powder*
*3/4 teaspoon Baking Powder*
*3/4 teaspoon Baking Soda*
*1/2 teaspoon Salt*
*1 Large Egg*
*1/2 cup Milk*
*1/4 cup Vegetable Oil*
*1 teaspoon Vanilla Extract*
*1/2 cup Hot Water*

## DIRECTIONS FOR PREPARING THIS RECIPE:

- Preheat your air fryer to 350F.
- Mix the first 6 ingredients in a large bowl. Then pour in the vegetable oil, milk, egg, and vanilla and mix well. Pour in the hot water and mix again.
- Let the mixture sit for 4 minutes.
- Coat the cake pan with cooking spray.
- Pour the batter into the pan and cover the top of the pan with aluminum foil. Poke holes in the foil.
- Place the pan in the basket of your preheated air fryer lower the temperature to 320F and set the timer for 35 minutes. After the 35 minutes, take the foil off the pan and cook for 10 more minutes. A toothpick placed in the center of the cake should come out clean when cooked.
- Let the cake cool for 10 minutes before serving.

By Alicia Patterson

# Baked Apple

Prep Time: 10 Minutes / Cook Time: 20 Minutes / Servings: 1
Use the Pizza Pan

## INGREDIENTS FOR MAKING THIS RECIPE:

1 medium apple
2 Tablespoon. chopped walnuts
2 Tablespoon. raisins
1 ½ teaspoon. butter, melted
¼ teaspoon. cinnamon
¼ teaspoon. nutmeg
¼ cup water

## DIRECTIONS FOR PREPARING THIS RECIPE:

* Preheat your air fryer to 355F.
* Slice the apple in half crosswise. Use a spoon to scoop out some of the inside.
* Mix the cinnamon, nutmeg, butter, raisins, and walnuts in a bowl.
* Spoon the mixture into the middle of the apple.
* Place the apple in piza pan. Put the water in the pan.
* Place the pan in the basket of your preheated air fryer and set the timer for 20.

Air Fryer Accessories Recipe Cookbook

# Shortbread Cookies

Prep Time: 10 Minutes / Cook Time: 20 Minutes / Servings: 2
Use the Pizza Pan

## INGREDIENTS FOR MAKING THIS RECIPE:

*250 g Plain Flour*
*75 g Caster Sugar*
*175 g Butter*
*1 Teaspoon Vanilla Essence*
*Chocolate Chips*

## DIRECTIONS FOR PREPARING THIS RECIPE:

- Preheat your air fryer to 355F.
- Place all the ingredients except for the chocolate chips in a big bowl and mix until a dough forms.
- Roll the dough out and use a cookie cutter to create whatever shapes you'd like.
- Place the cookies in the pizza pan.
- Place the pizza pan in the basket of your preheated air fryer and set the timer for 10 minutes.
- After the 10 minutes, lower the temperature to 320, place the chocolate chips on top of the cookies, and bake for 10 more a minute.
- Allow the cookies to cool for a few minutes before serving.

By Alicia Patterson

# Fried Banana S'more

Prep Time: 5 Minutes / Cook Time: 6 Minutes / Servings: 4

## INGREDIENTS FOR MAKING THIS RECIPE:

4 bananas
3 tablespoons mini semi-sweet chocolate chips
3 tablespoons mini peanut butter chips
3 tablespoons mini marshmallows
3 tablespoons graham cracker cereal

## DIRECTIONS FOR PREPARING THIS RECIPE:

* Preheat your air fryer to 400F.
* Slice the banana with the peels still on in half lengthwise, but don't cut down through the bottom peel and don't cut through the ends. Open the banana a little so that you have a pocket for the other ingredients.
* Fill the pocket with the remaining ingredients.
* Place the bananas in the basket of your preheated air fryer with the filling side up and set the timer for 6 minutes. The banana is cooked when the chocolate melts, the peel turns black, and the banana is soft.
* Allow the bananas to cool for a few minutes before serving.

Air Fryer Accessories Recipe Cookbook

# Mini Apple Pies

Prep Time: 10 Minutes / Cook Time: 18 Minutes / Servings: 9

## INGREDIENTS FOR MAKING THIS RECIPE:

75 g Plain Flour
33 g Butter
15 g Caster Sugar
Water
2 Medium Red Apples, peeled and diced
Pinch Cinnamon
Pinch Caster Sugar

## DIRECTIONS FOR PREPARING THIS RECIPE:

- Preheat your air fryer to 355F.
- Mix the flour and butter together. Then mix in the sugar. Slowly mix in water a tablespoon at a time until the mixture turns into a dough. Kneads the dough until it's smooth. Then use a rolling pin to roll it out
- Grease ramekins with butter.
- Cover the inside of the ramekin with dough. Then place an equal-amount of apples in each ramekin. Top with sugar and cinnamon.
- Put a layer of the dough on top of each ramekin. Use a fork to poke some hole in the dough.
- Place the ramekins in the basket of your preheated air and set the timer for 18 minutes. The banana is cooked when the chocolate melts, the peel turns black, and the banana is soft.
- Allow the pies to cool for a few minutes before serving.

By Alicia Patterson

# Chocolate M&M Cookies

Prep Time: 10 Minutes / Cook Time: 20 Minutes / Servings: 2
Use the Pizza Pan

## INGREDIENTS FOR MAKING THIS RECIPE:

*100 g Butter*
*100 g Caster Sugar*
*225 g Self Raising Flour*
*1 Teaspoon Vanilla Essence*
*5 Tablespoon Milk*
*3 Tablespoon Cocoa*
*1 bag of M&M's candy*
*50 g White Chocolate*

## DIRECTIONS FOR PREPARING THIS RECIPE:

- Preheat your air fryer to 355F.
- Put the sugar, cocoa, and flour in a bowl and combine until well mixed. Mix in the butter and then the vanilla.
- Break the white chocolate into small pieces and mix it in along with the milk in the cocoa mixture.
- Knead the dough until it becomes soft.
- Roll out the dough and cut out round cookies.
- Place half of the M&M's in the dough and half of them on top of it.
- Place the cookies in the pizza pan.
- Place the pan in the basket of your preheated air fryer and set the timer for 10 minutes.
- Allow the cookies to cool for a few minutes before serving.

Air Fryer Accessories Recipe Cookbook

# Pizza

By Alicia Patterson

# Pita Bread Cheese Pizza

Prep Time: 5 Minutes / Cook Time: 6 Minutes / Servings: 1
Use the Pizza Pan

## INGREDIENTS FOR MAKING THIS RECIPE:

*Pita Bread*
*1 Tablespoon Pizza Sauce*
*1/4 cup Mozzarella Cheese*
*1 drizzle Extra Virgin Olive Oil*
*1 Stainless Steel Short Legged Trivet*

*Toppings (optional):*
*7 slices Pepperoni or more*
*1/4 cup Sausage*
*1 Tablespoon Onions sliced thin*
*1/2 teaspoon Fresh Garlic minced*

## DIRECTIONS FOR PREPARING THIS RECIPE:

- Place the pizza pan in your air fryer and preheat your air fryer to 350F.
- Top the pita bread with pizza sauce, then cheese, and then toppings. Finish it off with a little drizzle of olive oil.
- Place the pita in the pizza pan in your preheated air fryer, and set the timer for 6 minutes.
- Cut the cooked pizza and Serve immediately.

Air Fryer Accessories Recipe Cookbook

# Caprese Pizza

Prep Time: 5 Minutes / Cook Time: 10 Minutes / Servings: 1
**Use the Pizza Pan**

## INGREDIENTS FOR MAKING THIS RECIPE:

*Mini pre-made 10" pizza crust*
*1 tomato, thinly sliced*
*1/4 cup Mozzarella Cheese*
*Handful of basil leaves, sliced*

## DIRECTIONS FOR PREPARING THIS RECIPE:

- Place the pizza pan in your air fryer and preheat your air fryer to 350F.
- Drizzle some balsamic vinegar on the pizza crust then top with cheese, basil, and a little more balsamic vinegar.
- Place the pizza in the pizza pan in your preheated air fryer, and set the timer for 8 to 10 minutes.
- Cut the cooked pizza and Serve immediately.

By Alicia Patterson

# Indian Spiced Turkey & Broccoli Pizza

Prep Time: 10 Minutes / Cook Time: 10 Minutes / Servings: 1
Use the Pizza Pan

## INGREDIENTS FOR MAKING THIS RECIPE:

*Mini pre-made 10" pizza crust*
*50 g Shredded Turkey Wing Meat*
*50 g Cooked Broccoli*
*3 tablespoons Cheddar Cheese*
*2 Tablespoons Homemade Tomato Sauce*
*1 Tablespoon Garam Masala*
*1 Tablespoon Mixed Spice*
*1 Tablespoon Coriander*
*Salt & Pepper*
*Fresh Basil*

## DIRECTIONS FOR PREPARING THIS RECIPE:

- Place the pizza pan in your air fryer and preheat your air fryer to 350F.
- Mix the coriander, mixed spice, garam masala, and turkey in a bowl.
- Coat the pizza crust with the tomato sauce then top with cheese, turkey, and broccoli. Add salt and pepper to taste, and sprinkle with basil.
- Place the pizza in the pizza pan in your preheated air fryer, and set the timer for 8 to 10 minutes.
- Cut the cooked pizza and Serve immediately.

Air Fryer Accessories Recipe Cookbook

# The Mafia Mangler Pizza

Prep Time: 5 Minutes / Cook Time: 10 Minutes / Servings: 1
Use the Pizza Pan

## INGREDIENTS FOR MAKING THIS RECIPE:

Mini pre-made 10" pizza crust
2 Tablespoon Pizza Sauce
1/4 cup Mozzarella Cheese
10 sliced Pepperoni
3 tbsp. diced ham
1 tbsp. black olives
Handful of mushrooms, sliced
½ tsp. black pepper

## DIRECTIONS FOR PREPARING THIS RECIPE:

- Place the pizza pan in your air fryer and preheat your air fryer to 350F.
- First, top the pizza with a layer of cheese on the base of the crust. Then add the pizza sauce, pepperoni, ham, mushrooms and black olives.
- Place the pizza in the pizza pan in your preheated air fryer, and set the timer for 8 to 10 minutes.
- Cut the cooked pizza and Serve immediately.

By Alicia Patterson

# The "Big Tony" Pizza

Prep Time: 5 Minutes / Cook Time: 10 Minutes / Servings: 1
Use the Pizza Pan

## INGREDIENTS FOR MAKING THIS RECIPE:

Mini pre-made 10" pizza crust
2 Tablespoon Pizza Sauce
1/4 cup Mozzarella Cheese
10 sliced Pepperoni
3 tbsp. diced ham
1 tbsp. black olives
Handful of mushrooms, sliced
½ tsp. black pepper

## DIRECTIONS FOR PREPARING THIS RECIPE:

- Place the pizza pan in your air fryer and preheat your air fryer to 350F.
- First, top the pizza with a layer of cheese on the base of the crust. Then add the pizza sauce, pepperoni, ham, mushrooms and black olives.
- Place the pizza in the pizza pan in your preheated air fryer, and set the timer for 8 to 10 minutes.
- Cut the cooked pizza and Serve immediately.

Air Fryer Accessories Recipe Cookbook

# The "Hot Meathead" Pizza

Prep Time: 5 Minutes / Cook Time: 10 Minutes / Servings: 1
Use the Pizza Pan

## INGREDIENTS FOR MAKING THIS RECIPE:

Mini pre-made 10" pizza crust
2 Tablespoon Pizza Sauce
1/4 cup Mozzarella Cheese
10 sliced Pepperoni
3 tbsp. diced ground beef
2 tbsp. diced ham
2 tbsp. cooked bacon
1 tbsp. black olives
Handful of mushrooms, sliced
½ tsp. Cayenne pepper

## DIRECTIONS FOR PREPARING THIS RECIPE:

- Place the pizza pan in your air fryer and preheat your air fryer to 350F.
- First, top the pizza with the pizza sauce. Then add the pepperoni, ground beef, ham, bacon, mushrooms and olives. Last...sprinkle on the Cayenne pepper (this stuff can get hot so know your heat tolerance!)
- Place the pizza in the pizza pan in your preheated air fryer, and set the timer for 8 to 10 minutes.
- Cut the cooked pizza and Serve immediately.

By Alicia Patterson

# What's Next On The List!

## Review Time... ☺

## PLEASE LEAVE US AN AMAZON REVIEW!

If you were pleased with our book then leave us a review on Amazon where you purchased this book! **Here's the web link to leave a review.**
**Simply type the link to your web browser,** scroll to the bottom & review!

### >>>  Amazon.com/dp/B07FK96P57   <<<

In the world of an author who writes books independently, your reviews are not only touching but important so that we know you like the material we have prepared for "you" our audience! So, leave us a review...we would love to see that you enjoyed our book!

If for any reason that you were less than happy with your experience then send me an email at **Info@RecipeNerds.com** and let me know how we can better your experience. We always come out with a few volumes of our books and will possibly be able to address some of your concerns. Do keep in mind that we strive to do our best to give you the highest quality of what "we the independent authors" pour our heart and tears into.

Hello all...I am very excited that you have purchased one of my publications. Please feel free to give us an amazon review where you purchased the book! If you already have, then I thank you for your many great reviews and comments! With a warm heart! ~Alicia Patterson "Personal & Professional Chef"

Air Fryer Accessories Recipe Cookbook

# Yours for Looking

## "BONUS" Get Your Air Fryer Marinades for Meats & Veggies Now!

**Get your very own Air Fryer Marinade Quick Start Guide!** This quick start guide will show you how to get the best tasting foods when cooking from your air fryer! **GET YOURS NOW** by just simply clicking the button below! **Enjoy!**

http://eepurl.com/dzsApr

By Alicia Patterson

Metric Volume, metric weight and oven temperature charts are tools that everyone wants in the kitchen, but are never around when you need them. That's why we have created these charts for you so you never skip a beat when you're cooking! Hope this helps! :)

# Metric Volume Conversions Chart

| US Volume Measure | Metric Equivalent |
| --- | --- |
| 1/8 teaspoon | 0.5 milliliters |
| 1/4 teaspoon | 1 milliliter |
| 1/2 teaspoon | 2.5 milliliters |
| 3/4 teaspoon | 4 milliliters |
| 1 teaspoon | 5 milliliters |
| 1 1/4 teaspoons | 6 milliliters |
| 1 1/2 teaspoons | 7.5 milliliters |
| 1 3/4 teaspoons | 8.5 milliliters |
| 2 teaspoons | 10 milliliters |
| 1/2 tablespoon | 7.5 milliliters |
| 1 tablespoon (3 teaspoons, 1/2 fluid ounce) | 15 milliliters |
| 2 tablespoons (1 fluid ounce) | 30 milliliters |
| 1/4 cup (4 tablespoons) | 60 milliliters |
| 1/3 cup | 90 milliliters |
| 1/2 cup (4 fluid ounces) | 125 milliliters |
| 2/3 cup | 160 milliliters |
| 3/4 cup (6 fluid ounces) | 180 milliliters |
| 1 cup (16 tablespoons, 8 fluid ounces) | 250 milliliters |
| 1 1/4 cups | 300 milliliters |
| 1 1/2 cups (12 fluid ounces) | 360 milliliters |
| 1 2/3 cups | 400 milliliters |
| 2 cups (1 pint) | 500 Milliliters |
| 3 cups | 700 Milliliters |
| 4 cups (1 quart) | 950 milliliters |
| 1 quart plus 1/4 cup | 1 liter |
| 4 quarts (1 gallon) | 3.8 liters |

Air Fryer Accessories Recipe Cookbook

# Metric Weight Conversion Chart

| US Weight Measure | Metric Equivalent |
|---|---|
| 1/2 ounce | 7 grams |
| 1/2 ounce | 15 grams |
| 3/4 ounce | 21 grams |
| 1 ounce | 28 grams |
| 1 1/4 ounces | 35 grams |
| 1 1/2 ounces | 42.5 grams |
| 1 2/3 ounces | 45 grams |
| 2 ounces | 57 grams |
| 3 ounces | 85 grams |
| 4 ounces (1/4 pound) | 113 grams |
| 5 ounces | 142 grams |
| 6 ounces | 170 grams |
| 7 ounces | 198 grams |
| 8 ounces (1/2 pound) | 227 grams |
| 12 ounces (3/4 pound) | 340 Grams |
| 16 ounces (1 pound) | 454 grams |
| 32.5 ounces (2.2 pounds) | 1 kilogram |

# Temperature Conversion Chart

| Degrees Fahrenheit | Degrees Celsius | Cool to Hot |
|---|---|---|
| 200° F | 100° C | Very cool oven |
| 250° F | 120° C | Very cool oven |
| 275° F | 140° C | Cool oven |
| 300° F | 150° C | Cool oven |
| 325° F | 160° C | Very moderate oven |
| 350° F | 180° C | Moderate oven |
| 375° F | 190° C | Moderate oven |
| 400° F | 200° C | Moderately hot oven |
| 425° F | 220° C | Hot oven |
| 450° F | 230° C | Hot oven |
| 475° F | 246° C | Very hot oven |

By Alicia Patterson

# Food Temperatures for Safe Heating, Danger Chilling & Freezing Zones!

*A guide for food temperature cooking!*

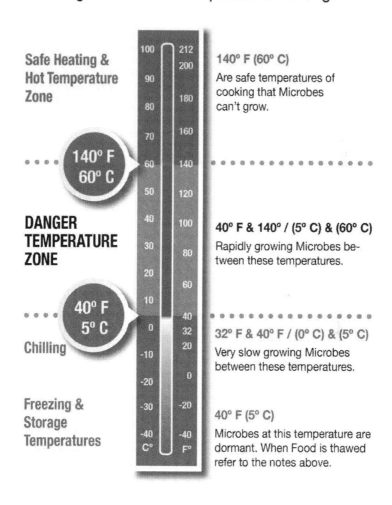

Safe Heating & Hot Temperature Zone

140° F (60° C)
Are safe temperatures of cooking that Microbes can't grow.

140° F
60° C

DANGER TEMPERATURE ZONE

40° F & 140° / (5° C) & (60° C)
Rapidly growing Microbes between these temperatures.

40° F
5° C

Chilling

32° F & 40° F / (0° C) & (5° C)
Very slow growing Microbes between these temperatures.

Freezing & Storage Temperatures

40° F (5° C)
Microbes at this temperature are dormant. When Food is thawed refer to the notes above.

Air Fryer Accessories Recipe Cookbook

# Air Fryer Creation Recipes & Notes:

**Create your very own "Marvelous Masterpieces".** Log all of them in this section. You will be amazed on how many ideas you come up with!
**Now get creating!**

| Name | Temp. | Time | Special Toppings or Glaze |
|------|-------|------|---------------------------|
|      |       |      |                           |
|      |       |      |                           |
|      |       |      |                           |
|      |       |      |                           |
|      |       |      |                           |
|      |       |      |                           |
|      |       |      |                           |
|      |       |      |                           |
|      |       |      |                           |
|      |       |      |                           |
|      |       |      |                           |
|      |       |      |                           |
|      |       |      |                           |
|      |       |      |                           |
|      |       |      |                           |
|      |       |      |                           |
|      |       |      |                           |
|      |       |      |                           |
|      |       |      |                           |
|      |       |      |                           |
|      |       |      |                           |
|      |       |      |                           |
|      |       |      |                           |
|      |       |      |                           |
|      |       |      |                           |
|      |       |      |                           |

By Alicia Patterson

# About The Author

Alicia Patterson is a southern girl from the heart of West Virginia that has a love for cooking in the kitchen. Growing up on a farm she quickly learned how to cook and prepare foods for a large family. Alicia started working at a restaurant and fell in love with it! Other restaurant owners soon learned how talented she was and she started teaching others how to cook like she did showing them how to enhance their menu items and pair foods together with their bar items, at the same time.

She has become a very well-known chef figure in the celebrity community. She has been working in the homes of many celebrities every-since. In her spare time she loves jogging, horseback riding and reading. And of course...her love in the kitchen is on the first of the list.

*"Hello and thank you for the purchase! I hope that this book captures your heart and give you more than enough ideas to what you can do with an air fryer!*
*Enjoy!" Alicia Patterson, xoxo*

Made in the USA
Coppell, TX
03 December 2019